TRADITIONAL
HOPI
KACHINAS

TRADITIONAL
HOPI
KACHINAS

A New Generation
of Carvers

Jonathan S. Day

NORTHLAND PUBLISHING

In memory of Ingvaya Quotskuyva. Hope the fish are bite'n.

www.northlandpub.com

The display and text type was set in Stone Print
Composed in the United States of America

Printed in Hong Kong

05   04   03   02   01   6   5   4   3   2

Day, Jonathan S., date.
    Traditional Hopi kachinas : a new generation of carvers / Jonathan S. Day.
       p.   cm.
    Includes bibliographical references and index.
    ISBN 0-87358-740-5 (alk. paper)
    1. Kachinas. 2. Hopi wood-carving. 3. Hopi wood-carvers–Interviews. I. Title.

E99.H7 D378 2000
745.592'21'0899745–dc21   99-051899

All portraits of artists by Jonathan S. Day, with the following exceptions: Jody Montgomery (page 23); Earl Denet (page33); Fred Ross (page 75); and Clark Tenankhongva (page 89). All photographs of katsina dolls by Rick Davis Photographic Communications, with the following exceptions: Klaus Kranz Photography (front and back cover, 10, 26, 32, 35, 102, 104, and 105) and the Museum of Northern Arizona (page 8). Photography on page vi (Janel Lomatewama), xiv, 16, and 106 by Owen Seumptewa; page 11 by Rick Davis Photographic Communications; page 27 by Tsakurshovi; page 45 by Barry Walsh; page 51 by Jonathan S. Day; page 57 by Barbara Rice; and page 83 by Ron Bergman. These photographs are copyrighted to the individual photographers or institutions.

COVER (LEFT TO RIGHT): *Larry Melendez,* TUSKYAPKATSINA *(Crazy Rattle); Philbert Honanie,* MANANG.YAKATSINA *(Collared Lizard); Manuel Denet Chavarria, Jr.,* KWASA'YKATSINA *(Black Dress). All Winter Sun Trading Company.*
BACK COVER (LEFT TO RIGHT): *Tay Polequaptewa,* KUWAN KOOKOPÖLÖ *(Assassin Fly) courtesy Daniel and Erin McCaffery; Fred Ross,* OWANGARORO *(Stone Eater), Winter Sun Trading Company; Manuel Denet Chavarria, Jr.,* HONÀN KATSINA *(Badger), Winter Sun Trading Company.*
FRONTISPIECE (LEFT TO RIGHT): *Manfred Susunkewa,* QÖÖQÖQLÖ *(no English translation); Manfred Susunkewa,* NANÀTSUVSIKYAVO *(Red Kilt Runner); Manfred Susunkewa,* SIVUTOOTOVI *(Black Fly). All Barbara Rice collection.*
PAGE III: *Ferris Satala,* HILILI *(no English translation). Barbara Rice collection.*

CONTENTS

FOREWORD

BY BARRY WALSH

Although the Hopi katsina religion dates back to to at least A.D. 1300, carvers have only been selling their dolls actively since about 1880. Since then, thousands of what are commonly referred to as katsina "dolls" have been created for Hopi use as well as for sale to anthropologists, collectors, and tourists. Despite the large number of dolls in existence, it is possible to speak of only about six distinctive styles of katsina doll and still be reasonably inclusive. Interestingly enough, the subject of this book is—in a sense— both the oldest and the most recent of these artistic developments: The New Traditional style katsina doll.

Helga Teiwes (drawing on Barton Wright) has discussed six basic styles of katsina carving in *Kachina Dolls: The Art of Hopi Carvers* (University of Arizona Press, 1991). I will briefly review these styles and Jonathan Day will approach them from a different slant in his introduction. The first katsina dolls were carved in the Early Traditional style, which appeared between 1880 and 1910. These dolls were flat or cylindrical in shape and very simple in form. Almost always painted with native mineral pigments, these dolls were carved with basic knives and sanded with sandstone or some other naturally occurring abrasive. Emphasis was on the face of the katsina figure. The body was often painted with the red three-stripe motif of the *putsqa tihu,* or cradle katsina. Hands and arms were barely represented on these dolls and the legs and feet were portrayed either not at all or using only a single cut to the base of the wood. The dolls had a string attached to their necks so that they could be hung on a wall.

Sometimes the Early Traditional dolls carried rather abstract hints of male or female genitalia. These anatomically correct dolls have been referred to as "pre-missionary," which is odd since missionaries were well-established and pursuing the Hopi long before these carvings were made.

OPPOSITE:
Hopi girls sometimes receive katsina dolls attached to wipho (cattails), which is a symbol of moisture.

Around 1910 and continuing into the 1930s, the Hopi began to produce a somewhat more refined type of doll referred to as the Late Traditional style. Although still largely cylindrical in shape, these dolls were more complex carvings. Arms and hands were brought out from the trunk of the doll and legs and feet were more fully formed and painted. The dolls took on a smoother appearance probably due to the availability of commercial sandpaper. Also, toward the end of the period, commercial paints in the form of tempera (or poster paint) were used for the first time. In many of the Late Traditional era dolls, the carver portrayed some basic details of the katsina's costume such as simple renderings of the sash, kilt, moccasins, and body paint.

By the end of World War II and into the 1950s, the Early Action style doll emerged. As the name suggests, these carvings were far more representational of the movements and actions of the katsinam as they danced. Thus, the Early Action style dolls were often carved with arms extended, feet spread, knees bent, one foot slightly upraised, and so on. These anatomical changes often resulted in the dolls being displayed on a base. Another development was that acrylic paints became available and were widely used—making for a brighter, sometimes shiny appearance. Greater detailing was added to the costumes of the dolls such as necklaces, armbands, and bowguards. A few of the carvers from this era began to have noticeably distinctive styles. Some even began to sign their dolls with initials or their full names on the base, a previously unheard of practice.

By the 1950s, the ever increasing number of tourists visiting Hopiland made katsina dolls a popular collectible. Not surprisingly, the Anglo visitor became convinced that if a detailed Early Action style katsina doll was good, it could nonetheless be better. How might it be "improved?" It was not a very imaginative step for buyers to "suggest" that katsina dolls be produced containing every detail of the katsina costume. Thus emerged the Late Action dolls with very precise depictions of fingers, toes, navels, and in some cases, potbellies and chin fat. Other features included glued-on bells for bandoliers and tiny stones in turquoise bracelets and necklaces. These dolls became increasingly viewed as "art objects" for which the artist's signature on the base of the doll was as important to the buyer as the quality of the katsina carving itself.

The logical progression of the Late Action katsina doll was to retain the exceptional attention to detail while increasing the realistic rendering of the subjects. So emerged the Modern Contemporary katsina carving in the late 1970s—an artistic trend that survives to this day. Most Modern Contemporary katsina dolls are all wood. Generally, they are painted in a new, more muted style, achieved by diluting professional oil paints or acrylics. The most distinctive feature of these Modern Contemporary dolls is their attention to detail, frequently taken to a level well beyond even the most precise of the Late Action figures. For example, Modern Contemporary dolls are carved to show individual strands of hair on the heads of katsinam and the threads on their garments. Wrinkles on knees and elbows are rendered with microscopic precision. This micro-detailing has become possible with the advent of new high speed electric wood-carving tools, which are expensive to buy and challenging to use. Another feature of these Modern Contemporary dolls is they often portray considerable dynamic movement including running, jumping, prancing, leaping, and the like. Some Hopi have complained that the Fine Art carvings of today portray katsina dancers in physical postures that no real katsinam ever assume. The implication has been that the tour de force nature of the artist—however impressive technically—may have gone too far.

Which brings us to the sixth type of katsina carving and the focus of this book. In the mid-to-late 1970s, a Hopi artist named Manfred Susunkewa was experiencing a mounting sense of discomfort. Noticing the increasing emphasis on technical virtuosity in katsina dolls, Susunkewa found himself feeling that "something important was being forgotten." Susunkewa remembered how katsina dolls looked when he was a child in the 1940s. He also recalled being in the kivas late at night for katsina dances in his native village of Songòopavi. His recollections of these times are not of beautiful costumes or exotic movements. Rather, his memories were of profound fear and respect, of awe and trepidation. Susunkewa wasn't sure that these deeply meaningful experiences were being conveyed by the Modern Contemporary katsina dolls.

Susunkewa decided to return to making katsina dolls in the old way, as only a few were still doing in the Hopi villages. His artistic efforts, along with those of anonymous carvers who kept the tradition alive, and a new crop of carvers featured in this book, have produced the sixth and most recent artistic trend in katsina doll carving: The New Traditional style katsina doll.

The interesting thing about the New Traditional style katsina doll is that it is both a new artistic development and a return to the old ways. As is shown in the many photographs provided in this book, the traditional-style dolls of today have many of the features of the old katsina carvings from 1880 to 1930. These New Traditionals are simply carved, cylindrical in shape, often painted with mineral pigments, and are meant to hang on the wall. They are intended to be simple expressions of the spirit of the katsinam, not precise renditions of their physical attributes.

While this might suggest that the traditional-style carvings of today are no more than replicas of the nineteenth-century dolls, this is not the case. The New Traditional style represents a new artistic movement in its own right that is firmly rooted in the old ways of making katsina dolls.

There are a number of features of the New Traditional style carvings that support their being viewed as a separate and distinct artistic style. First, the New Traditional style dolls are aesthetically different from their century-old cousins in a number of basic features. One need only put a number of antique dolls next to the New Traditional style dolls to note very obvious differences. These include marked contrasts in carving, sanding, and painting styles. Furthermore, the body proportions, posture, feet, and faces are distinctively different on the New Traditional style dolls.

The carvers represented in this book have emerged during the 1980s and 1990s with their own unique identifiable styles. The practiced observer can easily distinguish between carvings by Manfred Susunkewa, Clark Tenakhongva, Manuel Dénet Chavarria, Philbert Honanie, Vernon Mansfield, Bertram Tsavadawa, Spike Satala, and many others without checking for signatures or clan symbols. Having so many artists with distinctively different styles within a common tradition is but one indicator of a maturing art form. Another aspect is the increasing number of artists who are choosing to work exclusively in this style and to support their families by doing so.

While initially skeptical, the business world of Indian art is increasingly accepting the New Traditional style dolls. Many dealers in the Southwest and elsewhere are now specializing in or prominently featuring this style. In addition, there are numerous collectors who concentrate on acquiring New Traditional style dolls to the exclusion of the other five types of carvings discussed here.

Perhaps the ultimate confirmation of the new style comes from the Indian art establishment including major Indian art shows and museums. Many of the most prominent institutions (the Annual Santa Fe Indian Market, the Annual Hopi Show of the Museum of Northern Arizona, and the winter market of the Heard Museum) now offer annual prizes and awards in traditional-style katsina categories. Collections of the traditional-style dolls have also been featured in numerous museum exhibits.

A final comment concerns the author of this volume, Jonathan Day, better known as J. D. His father, Joseph Day, once told me a story about katsina dolls and J. D. that bears repeating. The story goes that Joseph and his first wife, the mother of J. D., were divorced years ago when J. D. was a very young boy. The result was that for most of each year, J. D. lived in Massachusetts about 2,500 miles away from his father. Based in Hopiland, Joseph would send his son a katsina doll each year around Christmas. And each year J. D. would hang the latest doll on his bedroom wall until he had acquired quite a collection. Now that cranky old trader, Joseph Day, would never admit it, but his intentions were clear in making these gifts. Joseph wanted his son to see the katsina dolls every day and think of him and Hopiland and all that the culture offers. This book serves as testimony that Joe's strategy was successful. Clearly, the carvings not only watched over J. D., but also eventually brought him to Hopiland, the source of the katsinam, and not incidentally, to his father. It is quite evident that the wisdom and beauty of Hopiland have had a central influence on J. D. He has written about the carvers and their dolls in a uniquely informal, appealing, respectful, humorous, and insightful way.

Read this book and you will see how quite some time ago those dolls on the wall spoke to J. D. And now it is J. D.'s turn to speak, sharing his voice with those of the katsina carvers and their carvings, whose messages bear close attention.

Dr. Barry Walsh is the Executive Director of The Bridge of Central Massachusetts, a human service agency. He is also the owner of Buffalo Barry's Indian Art in Worcester, MA. He is a collector and dealer in katsina dolls and has written numerous articles on topics related to katsina carvings.

Note from the Author

Though the Hopi spirit beings, and the dolls they give away when visiting Hopi, are commonly known as kachinas, in this book the spelling that more closely resembles Hopi pronunciation, katsina (plural katsinam) is used. There is no "ch" sound in the Hopi language.

In order to apply some standardization to the spellings of Hopi words, the names of the katsinam in this book are spelled in Third Mesa dialect using *Hopi Dictionary = Hopìikwa Lavàytutuveni: A Hopi-English Dictionary of the Third Mesa Dialect* (University of Arizona Press, 1998). However, the words may be pronounced differently on First Mesa or Second Mesa. Village names are also spelled in Third Mesa dialect, but the Glossary of Place Names on page 114 provides the English translation and meaning.

In addition, I left out any definitions for the functions of the katsinam. This book primarily focuses on the katsina dolls as art, and on the lives and philosophies of the artists; so I'll leave the definitions to someone else. In the back of this book you will find a list of many valuable books on the identification and function of katsinam. And, when you're in doubt, you may also quietly ask a Hopi.

Introduction

Respecting Hopi

I have had the privilege of learning about and visiting Hopi since I was a small child. As an Indian trader, my father traveled from village to village on business. He met a Hopi woman, settled down, and opened a trading post on Second Mesa. I learned about the business from them and eventually lived out every child's nightmare: I followed in my father's footsteps. I became an Indian trader.

Having been raised in this business has given me a great appreciation for Hopi art. I am fortunate to have witnessed things that few non-Indians will ever see, and I have often been accused of being an expert. "I know a lot for a white guy," I say, "but I really don't know anything." The reality is that the only way to be an expert on Hopi is to be born Hopi. Sure, my friends have shared much of their culture with me, but it is mostly superficial knowledge—knowledge obtained as a witness to a culture and not as a participant. My dad always says, "If I'm lucky they let me watch."

Hopis are often thought of as secretive and mysterious, but I think their quiet way is self-preservation in its truest form. So many outsiders have taken advantage of the Hopi—by spreading misinformation through books and seminars—that they are now reluctant to explain their culture and religion to non-Hopis.

The Hopi religion is a complex series of rituals and societies that includes a time table. That is to say, there are many things a Hopi doesn't learn until a certain age and there are many things a Hopi never learns. For instance, if a Hopi man is a member of the One Horn Society he has no idea what goes on in the Antelope Society. Secrecy guarantees that every Hopi religious society is important and irreplaceable. By the same token, no one Hopi knows everything or can speak for all Hopi. When an outsider writes a book and sacred things are revealed to the general public, this system is threatened, and the Hopi become wary of non-Indians. For this reason, it takes outsiders years to build trust and friendship with Hopis. I have learned many interesting things about Hopi culture and religion,

OPPOSITE:
The San Francisco Peaks loom majestically beyond the Hopi village of Walpi on First Mesa.

and I am very fortunate that this trust exists between many Hopis and myself. Therefore, out of my respect for Hopis, this book will focus on the complex lives of the artists and the beauty of their art form rather than on the Hopi religion. I wish to keep the trust the Hopi have in me intact and remain a trader, not a traitor.

STRANGER IN A STRANGE LAND

If you're driving on State Route 264 in northeastern Arizona, you just might miss the Hopi Mesas. Without the telephone poles dotting the mesatops the villages would be virtually undetectable. Their color and architecture blends perfectly with the landscape and are nearly hidden from the outside world.

However, people all over the world do know about the Hopi and are flocking to witness this culture and all the mystery it has to offer. Located ninety miles northeast of Flagstaff, the tribe numbers about ten thousand members and is completely surrounded by the Navajo Nation. Twelve villages nestle on or around First, Second, and Third Mesas. The Hopi have inhabited this area for more than a millennium, and many archaeologists believe that they are the true descendants of the Hisatsinom (Anasazi), as the Hopi have always claimed.

The high-desert climate is arid and inhospitable, but the Hopi thrive here. Over the years they have developed a complex religion to ensure their survival. They are primarily farmers—growing corn, beans, squash, and melons—and manage to survive on less than twelve inches of moisture a year. They use no irrigation or modern farming techniques. Instead, they rely on drought-hardy seeds, bred over a thousand years, and a lot of spiritual help.

Some help comes in the form of kachinas, or, more correctly, katsinam. These spiritual beings represent animals, plants, ancestors, and even neighboring tribes and have influence over everything from rain to specific plant growth. The katsinam are not gods, but supernatural beings who function as intermediaries or messengers between the Hopi and the ones who control the weather. Friends of the Hopi, they visit the villages and sing and dance prayers for moisture and the good of the world.

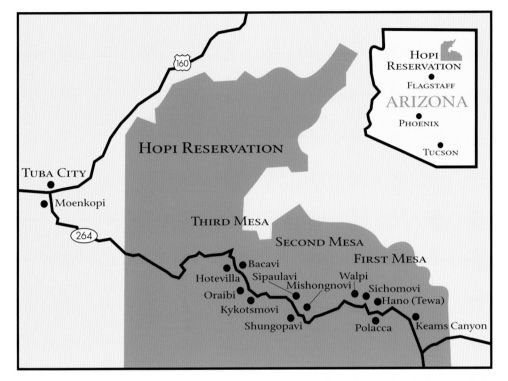

MAP OF HOPILAND *showing the Hopi villages. Note that spellings of village names reflect road signs and standard maps, not Third Mesa dialect.*

THE SAFEST PLACE IS THE NEAREST ROOFTOP

The Hopi live in sandstone villages where some buildings are eight hundred years old. In the center of each village is a plaza, or town square, surrounded by connecting homes. The homes are owned by different clans, and their windows and front doors face the plaza. One of the duties of owning a plaza home is opening its flat rooftop to spectators for plaza ceremonies.

From February through July, katsina ceremonies are held on a regular basis, some of which are open to non-Indians, or Pahaanas. Pahaana is a reference to a long-lost ancestor of the Hopi, an albino Hopi who set out on his migrations and never returned. When a scouting party from the Coronado Expedition arrived in 1540, the Hopi assumed that Don Pedro de Tobar, one of the party's leaders,

HOPI
CEREMONIAL
CALENDAR

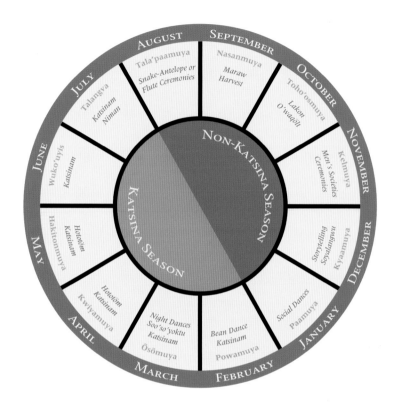

was their long-lost brother, Pahaana. Therefore, this has become the Hopi term for Anglos.

The ceremonies were once open to everyone because the Hopi are praying for the whole world, and therefore everyone should be welcome to attend. However, many of the dances have since been closed to non-Indians because some have treated sacred rituals as events staged purely for their benefit, which sometimes results in inappropriate behavior. Visitors have ignored simple rules such as no photography, and some have even applauded.

When a ceremony is closed there will usually be a sign at the entrance to the village or there may even be a police roadblock, so be prepared to be turned away. At other villages there may be no visible signs of closure, and you may not find out until someone eventually asks you to leave. Don't be offended. Just apologize and be on your way. There are plenty of other things to do and see at Hopi.

If you do attend an open ceremony be respectful. To illustrate this simple guideline I always ask people how they would conduct themselves if friends invited them to visit their church. Would you take a picture of the priest and interrupt to ask the significance of the wine and that smoking ball he's waving around? Of course not, and you should extend the same courtesy to the Hopi. Don't ask questions during a ceremony. You may inadvertently ask about something the six-year-old child standing next to you isn't supposed to know yet. If you need to ask a question, wait. Go to one of the local trading posts, make sure there are no children around, and quietly ask a Hopi. You may still not get the answer you want because there are some things Hopis feel you just don't need to know. Respect that, and enjoy the scenery.

A Hopi dance is one of the most spectacular events you will ever witness. When you enter a village during a ceremony, you will see a lot of people on the rooftops surrounding the plaza. That's where you should go, too. Traditionally the plaza is for women and children. In addition, the situation is always changing in the plaza. Katsinam are entering and leaving, and the clowns and disciplinarian katsinam are milling about. So, to guarantee that you're not standing in the wrong place when these changes occur, pick a roof with people on it and find the home's ladder. You don't need to ask permission. Just climb on up and take your cues from other Hopis who are standing quietly and watching the dance. (Remember to stand rather than sit because all of the seats and blankets are reserved.) This is the safest and the best way to enjoy the dance, and by "safest" I mean that it should keep the Hopi clowns (who just love to pick on non-Indians) from spotting you.

Hopi clowns function as examples of how not to be Hopi. Their antics often include political commentary and various staged events to show the Hopi what not to do. And yes, they love to single out Pahaanas. I remember one occasion in Kiqötsmovi when a few Pahaanas found themselves the center of attention at a katsina dance. A few weeks earlier, a Hopi had been caught selling religious items and artifacts to non-Indians, which served as the backdrop for one such event. The clowns called all the visitors off the roofs and into the plaza. They had arranged an auction of different items, a variety of things no one would want. One was a cow skull painted hot pink and adorned with feathers. Tacky at best, it still sold for thirteen dollars. The lucky bidder, thinking he had a great souvenir and story to take home, put the skull in his car and returned to watch the dance. But the story wasn't over yet. The next thing you knew,

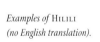

Examples of HILILI
(no English translation).

there was a Hopi policeman on the roof interrogating this guy about
the artifact he had in his car. The man was cuffed and put into cus-
tody. The police then drove into the center of the plaza in a squad car,
lights and sirens going, and brought out the culprit for trial. The
trial began after his accomplices (other clowns) were pointed out.
After a lengthy and hilarious trial the clowns were released and
the Pahaana convicted, sending the message that selling your culture
is not okay. The visitor wasn't allowed to keep the skull, but, for
being a good sport, he received more food than he could carry. So
beware, but don't worry too much. If you get pulled in, the most
you're going to get is really embarrassed.

Today, many dances are once again open to the public, but hik-
ing off paved roads is strictly forbidden. Many villages are even
closed to non-Indians altogether. One reason for village closures is
that archaeological sites, shrines, and other religious items have been
inadvertently damaged by unknowing tourists. Another reason is
privacy. People live here. An analogy my dad often uses is a backyard
barbecue. Picture a vanload of tourists pulling up to your house on
the Fourth of July and trampling in your bushes, looking in your windows, and taking pictures of your family. You'd call the police, right?

However, several villages are still open and some even have
guided tours. Just ask around and folks will be happy to give you
directions. You may also hire a Hopi guide who will make sure you
have a great time without any unfortunate consequences.

KATSINA DOLL STYLES

In the Southwest you will find hundreds of gift shops and trading
posts stocked with Indian art. One of the most popular items is the
katsin tihu (katsina doll). A *katsin tihu* is a carved representation of a
real katsina, made from *paako,* or cottonwood root, and adorned with
feathers. The plural of *katsin tihu* is *katsin tithu.* In traditional Hopi
culture these dolls are carved by the katsinam and given to young
girls and occasionally grandmothers. The easiest way to describe their
function is as a teaching tool. The dolls give the children a way to
remember a certain katsina—a way to learn its name, function, and
what it is supposed to look like. There are over five hundred different
katsinam. Variations in appearance occur even among the same kind

of katsina, depending on which village the katsina appears at. All of the katsina dolls pictured on page 6 represent a *Hilili,* a disciplinarian katsina that appears throughout Hopi. They all seem very different but share features common to all *Hilili,* even though they were carved by different artists. Try and pick out those features. This is a great way to hone your identification skills. Many people collect only variations of one kind of katsina.

Exactly when the first dolls were made available for sale is in dispute. However, most agree that by 1900, with some effort, you could get your hands on a Hopi katsina doll. These are often referred to as Early Traditional—simple, mainly flat dolls such as the one pictured to the right. This style is called a *putsqa tihu. Hahay'iwùuti* is the first doll given to an infant and is given in this flat doll form. In some Hopi villages it is also given to males. After the first doll, the girls continue to receive dolls over the years, while the boys receive traditional male toys (page 11). The age at which the gift-giving stops is up to the parents.

The cause of the katsina doll's evolution has generally been attributed to market demand and traders. Customers continued to demand more detail and that's what the traders ordered. The painting and the carving became more elaborate and the belly-acher style, or Late Traditional style, named for the way the hands hug the stomach, evolved. This style persisted for many years and the dolls gradually became more and more anatomically correct. Made popular in several mail-order catalogs, these dolls were the first to appear on the mass market and their availability ensured the continuation of the art form. They were very affordable (how does fifty cents sound?) and considered more a mysterious trinket than a work of art.

Beginning in the 1940s and continuing on into the 1950s, the Early Action style emerged. In addition to the added detail of the Late Traditional style, the Early Action style reflected some movement and were often displayed on a base of cottonwood root. Traditionally, katsina dolls are supposed to hang on a wall or from rafters. The cottonwood base was added purely so collectors could display them on bookshelves along with other collectibles. Modern acrylics also began replacing natural pigments and poster paints.

Manuel Denet Chavarria, Jr.,
Hahay'iwùuti
(no English translation).
Jonathan S. Day collection.

OPPOSITE:
unknown,
Mastopkatsina
(no English translation).
Museum of Northern Arizona.

LEFT:
William Quotskuyva,
ANGAKTSINA
(Long Hair).
Jonathan S. Day collection.

CENTER:
Kendrick Coochyamtewa,
POLII KATSINA
(no English translation).
Winter Sun Trading Company.

RIGHT:
Chris Timms,
KATSINMANA
(no English translation).
Winter Sun Trading Company.

In the late 1950s and early 1960s, the Late Action style, which is more familiar to most collectors, emerged. The action represented by the dolls increased so that they seemed frozen in motion, and the use of the cottonwood base became the norm. Cloth, yarn, and metal adorns this contemporary style, and more accurately resembles the real katsinam. Paving the way for the Modern Contemporary, the more detailed they became, the more they cost.

In the 1980s a completely different style was invented, the sculpture. Using the natural form of the root, an interpretive sculpture is carved. The top of the root consists of the complete face of a particular katsina, but the body is a free-form canvas for the artist. A combination of various Hopi symbols or a cliff-side village is common. This style continues to be made, but its popularity has dwindled during the 1990s.

The Modern Contemporary doll of the 1990s are generally carved from one piece of cottonwood root. A small hand-held drill called a Dremel is often used in addition to the knife and file. Wood burning is also a common technique to create details such as strands of hair. However, this method is frowned upon by some Hopi who believe that burning cottonwood root is like burning your children.

BOYS' GIFTS

THIS PHOTO ILLUSTRATES some of the gifts boys receive from the katsinam. The bow and arrow, called an *awta,* is the most common gift given to all boys at one time or another. Often during and after a ceremony you will witness   children chasing each other around the village shooting arrows at each other. The tips are made of wood and soon become blunt from hitting rocks and such. I remember that as a child I would re-sharpen them in a pencil sharpener, over and over again, until they were too short to shoot.

The next item is an *aya* (rattle). Boys often dance and mimic the katsinam with a bow in one hand and their rattle in the other, stomping their feet and singing made up songs, which loosely resemble those of the katsinam. The patterns on the rattles represent the four directions.

The odd-shaped, mustard-colored object is my favorite. Called a *tovokìmpi* (bullroarer), it is a piece of carved cottonwood root tied to a string. When you swing it around in a circular motion it roars with the sound of the wind though it sounds more like a helicopter. It's used to call in the rain clouds and they say that when someone uses it in the house it calls in the winds and sandstorms instead. The snakelike pattern on this *tovokìmpi* actually represents clouds and lightning.

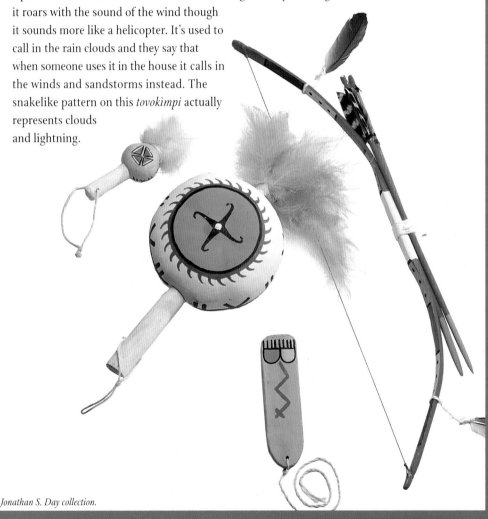

Jonathan S. Day collection.

In addition, the details that used to be made of yarn or fabric are carved on; even the feathers are carved on. The paints are acrylic or oil and the wood grain is often allowed to show through. This is the style most often seen in gift shops today. Their prices vary according to the artist but are generally fairly high. Prices range from eight hundred dollars to five thousand dollars for a superb piece.

THE NEW TRADITIONALS

The current style of belly-acher doll is referred to in this book as the New Traditional style or simply the traditional style. Some refer to these dolls as old style or new replicas, as if the Hopi stopped making them at some point. The reality is that the katsinam never stopped making them for ceremonial use, but Hopi artists stopped selling them in great quantity. Their demand dropped as interest leaned toward the ultra-realistic contemporary style.

Manfred Susunkewa,
HILILI
(no English translation).
Barbara Rice collection.

However, in the 1970s a Hopi artist named Manfred Susunkewa thought that the contemporary carvers were missing the point by making the katsina dolls look too pretty. He remembered growing up and seeing the old-style dolls on his sisters' walls and thinking that they weren't pretty at all. In fact, they frightened him, which was an amazing feeling for a child, and he wanted to recapture that emotional response. So, he carved a traditional-style doll and entered it in a show at the Heard Museum at a time when action dolls were the rage and won; the Heard purchased the doll for its permanent collection.

He is one of the few carvers who remembers when this style was still being given out and frequently sold. Often credited as being the first to revive this older style, Manfred notes that he remembers others doing it, but they had all passed away by the time he gave it a try. "It's almost like seeing a katsina dance in a kiva with kerosene lanterns," he said. "You could barely see. There was some primitiveness. I was looking for the ugliness of this medium that was practiced in the past."

Manfred manages to capture that primitiveness in a unique way. Because he was more of a witness to this style than most carvers, he cannot be compared with many New Traditional katsina carvers. He wasn't taught by someone else already doing this style, he reinvented it. Manfred is serious about carving these dolls and to him it involves not only spirituality, but also an appreciation and understanding of the past. "I'm not changing anything from the way my ancestors made them," he said. "The only thing that is different is time. I am carving old dolls today."

There have always been a few older Hopi who continued to make traditional dolls for sale, and younger generations are now following suit. Many want to preserve the old ways, while others just love the way the traditional style looks. Another appealing aspect of carving in this style is the decreased competition. There are probably over a thousand contemporary-style carvers, making it difficult for many artists to make a living. Still, even with the large number of carvers, the New Traditional style is the favorite at ceremonies. They are just more durable. Children are hard on their gifts and contemporary dolls are not designed for much wear.

I feel that the main appeal to the traditional style is that they more closely resemble the dolls in Hopi homes. The traditional-style dolls are as close as you can get to the dolls used in Hopi cultural life. Katsinam are supernatural beings, not humans; therefore the dolls should look otherworldly. Most are painted with mineral pigments and adorned with real feathers. They may also include leather, shells, horsehair, and fur. Most are not made from one piece of wood.

Along with katsinam, many Hopi also carve folk art. A nice break from the strict guidelines of a katsina doll, this offers the carver free reign on what he carves (see photo). Many pieces picture traditional Hopi life. These carvings are a rare find and sometimes the most interesting.

Overall, the traditional dolls are very diverse. Each carver has his own distinct carving and painting style. The more you look at these dolls, the easier it is to tell the artists apart at a glance. However, each artist is constantly evolving, and over time their work changes. One thing I have noticed that makes artist identification easier is the feet: Each artist has his own distinct way of carving them. It is almost to the point where this becomes the trademark and an

Manuel Denet Chavarria, Jr., FARMER. *Courtesy Tsakurshovi.*

Philbert Honanie,
FARMER.
Jonathan S. Day collection.

actual signature is unnecessary. After looking at a handful of dolls, you too will notice this unique quality. This comes in handy, as many of these artists sign their work intermittently. If you find you have bought an unsigned doll, you should be able to find someone who knows the maker's name based on the feet.

HOW TO COLLECT

Only the Hopi and Zuni make katsina dolls for sale with any frequency. Other Rio Grande pueblos practice a similar religion and make katsina dolls, but rarely offer them for sale.

Be sure the doll you buy is authentic. There are other local tribes producing similar-looking carvings, but they are not genuine katsina dolls. Most are made by minimum-wage employees in assembly-line fashion. Foreign imitations are also becoming prevalent. Authentic dolls have specific markings regardless of the maker. These special characteristics are something Hopis start learning at an early age. If a specific katsina doll is missing any of these characteristics it is considered incorrect and unsuitable for sale. Check the list of suggested reading in the back of this book for publications that can help you identify these characteristics. People who make imitations lack this knowledge and are therefore producing an inferior product. This production is also considered blasphemous by the Hopi, because the people making the imitations have no cultural or religious background in katsinam. As of yet, the Hopi have been unable to stop this practice, so here are a few suggestions.

WHERE TO BUY

Go to a reputable dealer. Reputable dealers will rarely give you more than 10 percent off anything, and if they do it's a real discount, actually cutting into their profits. If you choose to buy from the artist, I recommend buying on the Hopi or Zuni Reservations. Neither Hopis nor Zunis will sell fakes in their villages.

Make sure the clerk is knowledgeable by asking him or her straight out: "Is this made by a Hopi?" and "What's his name and what village is he from?" (The makers of the imitations aren't from any of the Hopi villages.) Most shops are on a first-name basis with their artists and buy from a select group of Hopi they have developed a relationship with over the years. In addition, merchants should know a fair bit about the names and functions of the different katsinam. They should be able to tell you a lot about the doll you're looking at.

BUYER BEWARE

Watch out for certificates of authenticity. I have never seen a genuine katsina doll come with one. If the doll has a cape or kilt made of vinyl, check underneath for nails. Nails haven't been used in Hopi dolls for more than fifty years. The Zuni occasionally use them, but only as a means of allowing the limbs to move. The kilt on imitations is usually made out of vinyl and painted with magic markers. Hopi dolls, as I mentioned, are made of cottonwood root, which is almost as light as balsa wood. The imitations are generally made out of pine. Pick up the doll—its light weight should surprise you. However, remember that there are exceptions. Once in a while a carver can't find a choice piece of cottonwood root and will carve out of a heavier piece. That's why it's important to go to reputable dealers: They can weed out the fakes for you.

BUY WHAT YOU LIKE

There is an old saying in this business: "If you like it, buy it, because you'll never see it again." I can't stress this point enough. I have heard too many regretful stories from people who wished they had made a particular purchase. Two years later they find themselves searching for that special doll they saw somewhere on Second Mesa. Remember, every piece is one-of-a-kind and inevitably sells by the time you return to buy it. In addition, don't buy dolls based on rarity or the name on the bottom. Buy it because you love it. Regardless of the artist, a Hopi katsina doll rarely goes down in value. In the long run, I think a doll you purchase from a famous carver for no other reason than the fact that he is famous makes that doll less valuable than one you really love whether the carver is famous or unknown.

THE
ARTISTS

BENDREW ATOKUKU

I noticed Bendrew peeking out from under the hood of his truck when I pulled into his driveway. "Do you have a good battery in that thing?," he said with a smile. "I need a jump." After numerous attempts to get his truck up and running we finally gave up. I put my reservation mutt, your typical brownish ranch dog mix, in the back of my truck and went inside.

A member of the Water Clan from Songòopavi, Bendrew has spent his entire life on the reservation, with the exception of the time he spent in Flagstaff during high school. Born two months prematurely at Phoenix's St. Joseph's Hospital, he weighed in at a mere two pounds, three ounces. He and his mother stayed at the hospital for several months until he was healthy enough to come home. That's about the extent of his travels. He was raised in a traditional home in his village and now lives in Tuba City with his wife Renee.

"I'm what you call F.B.I.—full-blooded Indian."

When Bendrew was in fifth grade, his father taught him how to carve. Like his father, Bendrew tried the contemporary style, but quickly moved on to sculptures. He continued to carve them for many years until Philbert Honanie (page 36) introduced him to the traditional style in 1993. Philbert taught him about pigments and tying feathers, knowledge he would later pass on to clan brother Clifford Torivio (page 94).

"Clifford came by to visit," Bendrew said. "He had made a nice contemporary *Sa'lako*. It was pretty cool, but he was bored with the style. So I said, 'Sit down and try this old style.' A week later, he came down and started carving. I showed him how to mark and cut it out, and later I showed him how to make his paints. He's just been tearing it up ever since."

Bendrew has been "tearing it up" as well. He sold his first doll to Tsakurshovi (page 27), a trading post on Second Mesa. It was a *Maakkatsin*, a hunter, probably about five inches tall. Bendrew made

OPPOSITE LEFT:
MANANG.YAKATSINA
(Collared Lizard).

OPPOSITE CENTER:
OWAK KATSINA
(Coal Katsina).

OPPOSITE RIGHT:
YÖNGÖSON KATSINA
(Tewa Turtle Katsina).
All Jonathan S. Day collection.

PAGE 16:
A quiet path wends its way toward Hotvela and its terrace gardens.

fifty dollars. Today, you can find his work in several Arizona galleries including Winter Sun Trading Company (page 87) and Tsakurshovi. His outgoing, friendly personality has helped him build relationships with many shop and gallery owners.

The staccato gunfire of video games filled the living room as Bendrew's son played Nintendo on the floor in front of us. Sitting on the couch, I noticed a beat-up *putsqa tihu* resting on a nearby hutch. Bendrew picked it up and showed it to me. It was his one-year-old daughter's first doll: a *Hahay'iwùuti*, which was missing most of its paint and showing a lot of teeth marks. In a strange way, he seemed proud that his daughter had done so much damage. This is an important difference between contemporary and traditional-style dolls—children play with them.

"When you're carving the feathers real thin and real fine," Bendrew says, "you'll sometimes chip it and have to repair it. When I'm carving a traditional-style doll I'll be piecing it together and I'll accidentally drop it and nothing will break and I'll say, 'All right, tough doll. You'll be strong for years to come.'" After many years Bendrew still finds the traditional style more satisfying to create.

*"We started out with these [traditional-style dolls]
first. That's how they looked a long time ago. I'm just
trying not to let it go away."*

Bendrew feels that the traditional style's nostalgic appeal is universal and attracts Hopis and non-Indian buyers alike. "It was the first kind of art that came out at Hopi," he says. Everything's natural, from the earth: the pigments, the wood, and the feathers.

How Hopi children view katsinam is also very important to Bendrew. He feels that the children should be exposed to traditional-style dolls. "[Contemporary-style carvers] try to make everything detailed, the way it really looks. That kind of messes it up for us, for the kids. [The contemporary-style dolls] show the chin or the ears. It's too human."

According to Bendrew, the significance of each doll is important, and the traditional style relays more of that to the buyer. The muted colors and exaggerated anatomy relay something more mysterious and spiritual. "They all have different meanings from within the earth and outside of the world: the rocks, the sand, the insects, the animals, stars, even the planets and the sun. They have more meanings than anything else in Hopi."

We talked at length about the spiritual aspect of Hopi, the closing of the ceremonies to non-Indians, and the non-Indian influence on Hopi. "If they can come out and just watch it [a katsina dance] and not take pictures, it's okay. If they respect us, we'll respect them back and be friends." And even though Bendrew installs satellite systems when he's not carving, he feels that some television programs and books about the Hopi do more harm than good. The television and video games distract children from a traditional way of life. He also noted that some books accidentally expose children to information they're not supposed to know yet.

Today, Bendrew continues to carve in Mùnqapi (Moenkopi), Arizona, where he lives with his wife Renee and their children. Eventually they plan to move to Renee's house in Kiqötsmovi. The funny thing is that this is the same sandstone house I used to dream about when I was a child. Everytime I passed it on the way through K-Town I hoped to someday live in a house like that. Ironically, it took all these years to find out that the house is owned by friends.

LEFT:
PÖQANGWHOYA
(Warrior Twin).
Jonathan S. Day collection.

RIGHT:
ANGAKTSINA
(Long Hair).
Winter Sun Trading Company.

Manuel Denet Chavarria, Jr.

Manuel lives in a little rock house at the bottom of First Mesa. He's one of the few Hopis I know who collects antiques; his house reminds me of an old trading post. Display cases dot his living room and in the corner stands his work area. Stacked against the wall are pieces of wood and on his work table sit dolls in progress. This is the infamous table Manuel and I used to joke about when I worked at Winter Sun. He would bring in a doll for sale and I would try to place it on the shop's glass display case. Despite my best efforts, the doll would fall over every time. Manuel would laugh and say, "It stands on my table!" His table is so warped and caked with paints that even the most unbalanced doll could be positioned somewhere.

Though he lived in Phoenix when he was younger, weekends and school breaks were always spent at Hopi. As a child he stayed with his relatives, the Secakukus, who owned a grocery/hardware/trading post/gas station at the bottom of Second Mesa, which is no longer there. From the age of ten until his late teens you could find Manuel working there.

"I didn't get paid, but I got credit in the store," Manuel said. "I could sign for stuff and that was good enough for me." In addition to the store credit, the job provided Manuel a glimpse at life beyond the reservation. "It was cool! I always liked pumping gas, because you met all the people passing through."

Manfred Susunkewa was the first New Traditional style carver that influenced Manuel, but he also remembers seeing old-style dolls in the trading post when he was a boy. He began carving when he was thirteen, and he started with corn dolls: cylindrical dolls with the bodies painted as corn and the faces painted as various katsinam.

"I used to sell action dolls to the Heard and other
traders in Phoenix when I was about fifteen, but
I never really did very good with them."

OPPOSITE LEFT:
Hehey'a
(no English translation).
OPPOSITE CENTER:
Nata'aska
(Black Ogre).
OPPOSITE RIGHT:
Hakto
(no English translation).
All Barbara Rice collection.

Another influence was Otille Jackson, the first female contemporary-style carver. When Manuel experimented with full-figure action dolls, she gave him advice and encouragement. According to Manuel, her best advice was, "Never leave home without your tools. You can go anywhere and sell these." This advice came in handy while Manuel was in the army. Stationed at Fort Knox, Kentucky, he and some friends decided to take a road trip. "I was going on a weekend trip to Indianapolis, and I was kind of short on money. So I took three dolls with me. If I didn't sell them it was going to be a bummer. I had no idea where I was going to sell them. I tried one number: Haggards' Trading Post. They said, 'Come on over.' They were treating me so good, giving me coffee, inviting me to dinner. It was like I went home or something. I traded a little and got some cash for those dolls."

After that meeting, Manuel figured he would never see the Haggards again. But in 1990, Manuel's wife, Marlinda, was working at the Monongya Gallery on Third Mesa. While talking to a couple from Indianapolis, she mentioned that her husband had been in the service at Fort Knox. The connection was made; they were the Haggards. To this day they are still in contact. Manuel says they have some of his best work.

SOWI'INGWKATSINA
(Deer Katsina).
Winter Sun Trading
Company.

When Manuel moved permanently to Hopi in the 1980s, he was still carving the contemporary style. Then a new store opened on Second Mesa and Manuel went there to sell his dolls. The shop was Tsakurshovi (page 27) and, at that time, they had very few dolls, but three of them happened to be Manfred Susunkewa's.

"They [Manfred's dolls] were just real different, real funky looking, and I liked them."

At the owner's suggestion Manuel decided to give the traditional style a try. "I had a flat piece and started carving on it that evening and got it done in the middle of the night sometime. I carved out a *Koyala,* a Tewa clown katsina, all one piece, painted it and everything. I went to sell it the next day and Joseph [the store's owner] paid me eighty dollars and that was it. I started carving traditional." Manuel's carvings were different in those days. "At first I was going for that reproduction-type doll. I didn't want it to look like a new doll in the old style. I wanted it to look like an antique. I was doing different work than I'm doing now."

In the beginning, the response at Hopi was mixed because the style was just emerging. "During my first couple of years I received some negative responses from Hopis. Then I went around to my grandmother and other older family members and asked them for their advice. I didn't know if what I was doing was right or wrong and they said it was okay and they liked what I was doing, especially my grandmother. She really liked them." That was all the reassurance Manuel needed.

He entered his first show at the Museum of Northern Arizona, where he won second and third place, and two honorable mentions. Manfred Susunkewa won first that year.

Since that first show, Manuel continues to excel. He's won more awards than I can count and has been featured in *Arizona Highways* magazine, Jerry and Lois Jacka's *Art of the Hopi* (Northland Publishing, 1998), and many other publications. Manuel now garners positive recognition at shows and by art enthusiasts, but this wasn't always the case. "There's a lot of interest in it now; it's not a quiet, little secret anymore. Now when I do shows, I don't spend all my time educating people about it. I just mention it and they already know. Before, I used to have to talk so much just to sell one doll. Going to shows and coming home with no money was a regular routine."

> *"I try to take it slow. I want to get old and be carving
> this style, and I want the style to continue to grow."*

Manuel is thrilled that he can support his family by doing something he loves. "There aren't any decent jobs out here that you can raise a family on. It's just a hassle when you have a job. I feel being an artist gives me religious freedom. That's why I feel real fortunate. This is a way I can support my family and still be free to do other things."

PALHIKWMANA
(Moisture Maiden).
Gary and LeeAnn Wilhelmi collection.

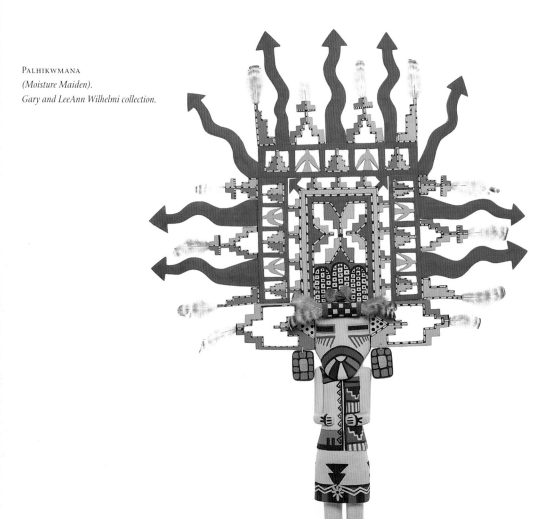

Manuel also likes the fact that the style's popularity is still in its infancy. Traditional dolls are readily available, but the number of makers is small compared to the contemporary carvers. This means opportunity and longevity. "You see the potential. It's like an open field. In the traditional style there's not all these guys at the top, and you can't fight your way up. If you do good work and are consistent you can excel."

JOSEPH AND JANICE DAY
TSAKURSHOVI

ON TOP OF SECOND MESA just outside of Songòopavi is a little shop called Tsakurshovi. If you have a sense of humor and want to purchase some of the finest art available, it's a stop on the reservation that shouldn't be missed. Joseph first visited Hopi in 1970 as a slack-jawed tourist out to see a ceremony. By 1980 he and his Hopi wife, Janice, were wholesaling Indian art, and in 1988 they decided to break into retail. In the early days, they financed the construction of the shop by selling the now-infamous "Don't Worry, Be Hopi" T-shirts from the back of their 1966 Volvo at the Hopi Cultural Center. Thousands of T-shirts later, they run one of the last old-time trading posts, a place where you can not only buy a great traditional-style doll but can also pick up pigments, fox pelts, macaw feathers, and gourds. Tsakurshovi is one of the few stores where the Hopi shop; probably half their business is with the locals. Where else can you buy *tuuma* (white clay), Hopi *sakwatootsi* (Hopi blue moccasins), and *honngàapi* (bear root)?

Joseph and Janice are major players in the revival of the traditional style among the younger carvers. "I collect and sell traditional-style dolls because they say something important about Hopi culture that dolls carved for the non-Hopi market do not. More dolls are now being carved for non-Hopi consumption, which means that the non-Hopi art market dictates the style and, as a result, that style is moving increasingly away from its Hopi cultural context." Though he does sell some contemporary dolls he believes traditional is really the way to go. "Most contemporary dolls are about technique, craftsmanship, human anatomy, and gratuitous action, while traditional dolls are about capturing the essence of a particular spirit, and that is why traditional-style dolls are more successful as art."

DANNY DENET

Just from the decor at his sister's house I could tell Danny had an interesting family. His father's military burial flag, wrapped in plastic, hung on the wall above the recliner where Danny sat. All around the house, art and photographs of varying tribal origins, including Tewa pottery and Hopi katsina dolls, hinted at his unique cultural background.

A mix of Laguna, Hopi, and Navajo, Danny was born in a naval hospital in Orange County, California. His father was a career marine, which kept the family traveling until Danny was sixteen. He carved his first doll at fifteen while living in North Carolina. His father wanted him to learn about his heritage even though he didn't grow up Hopi. The doll was an old-style *Yehoho,* a Laguna-style corn boy that appears at Hopi. His grandmother still has the doll in her house at Sitsom'ovi.

Danny has tried to learn about each side of his family, but doesn't know any of the languages well. "There's too many to learn," he said. His mother, a full-blooded Laguna, was adopted into the Hopi Sun-Eagle Clan at First Mesa over thirty years ago; his father is half Navajo and half Hopi. Danny remembers that it was harder for his father to be of mixed ancestry when he was a young man. "My father felt that he had to do everything twice as good and learn everything twice as fast as the other men, in order to prove himself to be a Hopi at heart." It was this prejudice that eventually led his father to join the Marine Corps and leave Hopi. Today, Hopis are less concerned with differences and Danny has found only acceptance at Hopi.

OPPOSITE LEFT:
TUNGWUP TAAHA'AMU *(Whipper's Uncle).*
OPPOSITE CENTER:
HONÀN KATSINA *(Badger).*
OPPOSITE RIGHT:
SIPIKNITAQA *(Zuni Warrior).*
All Barbara Rice collection.

Danny lived at Laguna briefly and even danced powwow in Winslow, but he is most familiar with the Hopi ways. When he was seventeen he moved back to Hopi and often traveled with his family to shows throughout the Southwest. He took up carving again, this time in the contemporary style. Just about everyone in his family was an artist and his father had even attended art school.

It wasn't until Danny's cousin, Manuel Denet Chavarria, Jr., (page 22) started carving the traditional-style dolls that he became interested in them. "We'd be at our house in Polacca: Junior (Manuel), my dad, my neighbors, and all the other guys. We'd sit around and carve all day and just talk." Everyone seemed to like the new dolls but were hesitant about their marketability. Danny is quick, however, to credit his father with helping the boys really get started with them. "At first he was against it because he didn't think it would sell. Once he saw that we could sell them he said, 'Okay, let me show you some little tricks.' He helped us tie our feathers and showed us how to get certain colors. 'This is how we used to do it,' he said. Instead of using wood we could use corn husks, leather, sheepskin, and yarn. He showed us all that stuff."

"I usually carve the ones that still come out.
The ones that I see dancing."

Still, Danny continued to make the contemporary dolls and Manuel continued with the traditional. Danny, however, found he was having trouble making ends meet. "I didn't have a job and I had my first child. I couldn't support my family because it takes three to four weeks to finish a doll. I could make the old style a little faster, so I started carving one doll contemporary and a few old style, and that was enough to get me through the month." I remember seeing those first dolls; we used to joke and call them boxers. Danny carved the hands so round and large they looked as though they were wearing boxing gloves, a unique style that sets him apart from other carvers and adds to the diversity of the art form. Today, his traditional dolls are some of the best around.

He found this new style enjoyable to carve and more pleasing to the eye. "What I like about them is the way they look. They look more authentic than some of these contemporary dolls. Contemporary dolls are more scary; you don't want dolls like that. They seem like they could come alive, and they're not supposed to. They're supposed to be there for the kids."

In the beginning, Danny and his cousins sold mostly to tourists,

MOSAYURMANA
(Buffalo Maiden).
Barbara Rice collection.

from a relative's house right on the mesa top. Tourists reacted favorably, but they were sometimes confused at first glance. "Most of the time we just had them hanging on the wall and they [tourists] thought they were stuff we got for the kids. So we told them, 'No, these are for sale.' They were really surprised. They thought they were old dolls." Danny said it was a lot of fun meeting people, making them feel welcome, occasionally inviting them to his grandmother's for dinner.

> *"They really liked the traditional style. It was*
> *something they hadn't seen before and most of*
> *the tourists were looking for something original."*

PALHIKWMANA
(Moisture Maiden).
Winter Sun Trading Company.

Now living in Flagstaff, Danny works a regular nine-to-five job with a periodicals distributor and carves in his spare time.

Like everything, art goes in cycles. Soon, when he moves back to the Hopi Reservation, we'll see a lot more of Danny's work. He wants to move onto the Hopi-partitioned land with his family, build a little house, and relax. A little place in the country—isn't that what everyone wants?

EARL DENET

On their way to go fishing, Manuel and Danny Denet's older brother, Earl, stopped by my house. I had never met Earl, but the resemblance to his brother is remarkable. When I saw him walking up my drive-way with a box full of dolls I thought to myself, "I wonder what Danny is doing here." Even their voices are similar.

Like his brother, Earl traveled around the country with his family until their father retired from the military. They settled on the Hopi Reservation and Earl gave carving a try. His grandfather gave him some money to go buy his first piece of wood. When he was ten he started carving in the traditional style, but carved only a few dolls. His interest in carving didn't resurface until he was almost out of high school.

After graduation Earl decided to take a trip to Utah. His future wife, Althea, had moved to Salt Lake City and Earl wanted to help her settle in. He was only going to stay for two weeks, but he never returned. He began attending a community college and, after earn-ing his associate's degree, found a job at a local semiconductor plant. He's been working the night shift there ever since. He and Althea eventually married and now have four children.

Earl continued to carve in his spare time and his mother-in-law began selling his work for him at Hopi. At one time she rented out rooms in her house to tourists and often entertained tour groups. They would tour First Mesa and then eat a home-cooked Hopi meal. She mentioned to Earl that they were always looking for dolls, and suggested he send them to her. "So I'd send her stuff to sell every once in a while. I never really got out and did shows." Earl sells much of his work in Salt Lake City; he also frequents powwows and says they are good marketplaces as well. He pays his kids a com-mission on anything they sell.

His favorite katsina to carve is *Kookopölö* (Kokopelli). "I carve it the most and I like to get it looking different every time," he said. "I

OPPOSITE LEFT:
HUUHUWA
(Cross-legged Katsina).
OPPOSITE CENTER:
PALHIKWMANA
(Moisture Maiden).
OPPOSITE RIGHT:
KOOKOPÖLÖ
(Assassin Fly Katsina).
All Earl Denet collection.

get different pieces of wood and work with that." Earl appreciates the simplicity of the traditional style and recalled seeing even more simplistic dolls at his mother's village of Paguate at Laguna.

"This is the old tradition. These are what the dolls looked like before any major white influences came."

Earl only carves a few hours a night. "It's only a hobby for me," he said. "I like that I can finish a traditional doll in a few weeks, whereas the contemporary, I tried but never finished them. I have three or four of them still sitting around. I may never finish them. With the traditional style I saw that I could carve and see a finished product."

He learned a lot from his relatives but has developed that knowledge into his own style. "Manuel showed me the paints. I would go out and visit and I would pick up things. He was usually carving when I would come by. I'd just watch him and he would show me some stuff."

Though he loves Utah, Earl misses Hopi, and continues to visit about every other month. "We come out more now for my kids," he said. "This is their time to learn, and I know what I missed when I was their age. I know that they need to be out here and I'll learn along with them now." An avid fisherman, he uses that solitary time not only to gather carving wood but also to remember his roots. "That's the way I keep close with my culture, being so far away. I sit down and start thinking about things at home. Try to remember things." Carving traditional-style dolls is one way that he becomes closer to his culture.

Earl believes that the rich culture and religion is the draw for non-Indians and has mixed feelings on the closure of some ceremonies. "I was always told that the katsina dances are for everyone. For that reason I feel like they really shouldn't be closed. I don't blame them for closing the dances though, because I know how disrespectful some people can be." Earl looks forward to the day that everyone respects the Hopi religion and that all the dances may once

again be open to the public. "Visitors tell me it's the spirituality of Hopi. They go out there so they can feel spiritual."

For now Earl continues to carve in his spare time, but you may find his work if you're ever at a powwow in Salt Lake City. Occasionally, you may also see some of his carvings in Arizona.

Philbert Honanie

Philbert Honanie is a member of the Coyote Clan at Hotvela. He told me to drop by his mother's house to chat. When I arrived, Philbert, his family, and some of his friends were in the living room. His wife was in the other room with friends weaving a basket for an upcoming ceremony. The kitchen table was stacked with boxes of fried chicken, biscuits, and mashed potatoes from the Kentucky Fried Chicken over sixty miles away in Tuba City.

Philbert was born on the reservation, but he also spent some time in Cedar Rapids, Iowa. He was placed in foster care when he was nine and remained there for almost three years. "I thought I was going to a place where I was going to be educated and straightened out, to where I wasn't going to become what I was intended to be. It was hard at first. I didn't have any place to go hunt or go running around. So it was a different atmosphere than what I was used to. It was like going through a time warp."

Racism also had an impact on this difficult period in Philbert's life. "I had friends, but they couldn't really cope with me because I was an Indian. They were all white and they wanted to hang out with whites." He was thirteen when he moved back to Hopi. His mother was living in Phoenix, so he moved in with his grandmother.

He met his wife when he was eighteen and they had their first child soon after. They now have three children and have been together since the mid-80s, which is about how long Philbert's been carving.

He started by selling sculptures on his own at the Hopi Cultural Center and then moved on to retail stores. Sculptures were all the rage in the 1980s, and Philbert still makes them occasionally for special orders. In the late 1980s he started experimenting with traditional-style dolls. He used to hang out at Tsakurshovi (page 27) on Second Mesa, and with the encouragement of the owner, gave it a shot. He loved the colors, and says that to this day it's the colors that keep him going. "It's all-natural, it's not too bright, and it's not too glamorous. It's just perfect." While his skills continued to improve, more opportunities became available. Philbert's work

OPPOSITE LEFT:
Kuwan Kookopölö
(Fancy Assassin Fly).
Winter Sun Trading Company.

OPPOSITE CENTER:
Angwusnasomtaqa
(Crow Mother). Basket of corn
seeds detail shown below.
Barbara Rice collection.

OPPOSITE RIGHT:
Masawkatsinmana
(no English translation).
Jonathan S. Day collection.

started appearing in more galleries and he was being invited to all the big shows. He's even gone as far as Hawaii for a one-man show in a private gallery, but he still credits traders like Phyllis Hogan (page 87), Barry Walsh (page 45), and Joseph Day (page 27) for their help.

"The traditional style is the reality of what a katsina is really about and what I'm really about. That's what I like about it."

Philbert told me about respect as he busily fixed up a pair of white moccasins for a friend. He had already coated them with *tuuma,* and was now scratching and slapping them to remove any excess. Philbert takes carving very seriously. He believes that each doll embodies the spirit of that katsina and treats them accordingly, going so far as to insist that they be carved to completion at Hopi and not off the reservation. "I talk to my dolls while I carve. I love them all. If I'm carving something that is rarely carved I say, 'I'm not trying to hurt you or anything; I know you're going to have a good home. Just give me this opportunity to live off you so I can care for my family.'" This respect has been learned over many years.

This kind and respectful attitude is what makes Philbert so popular. He is a genuinely nice guy, happy to share his fried chicken and make you feel at home. He believes life has a lot of lessons in store for us and learning them initiates change, which makes you a better person. He tells this story about an occasion when he was carving a doll and wasn't being very careful:

Masawkatsina
(no English translation).
Jonathan S. Day collection.

> I was in a rush and I dropped that doll about three times. It was almost finished and I broke him in different places. I was frustrated and threw that katsina doll away. After that I spent half of the rest of the day just carving, but something kept telling me: 'Get that doll out of there, get that doll out of there.' Finally I said, 'Okay, there is something I have to get clear here.' So I went back and pulled that doll out and I looked at it, and you could tell the doll didn't feel good. You could tell in the doll's face and eyes. So I glued it back together and hung it up on the wall. The next day I fixed it up, and

sold it right away, and the person really loved it. I knew that it wanted to go. I learned to respect my work and take my time. If I don't take things right, in time, and I try to make things move too fast, things aren't going to work out.

"It's not just an art form. It's a tradition. It's spiritual.
They say one of these days when you pass away you're
going to become a katsina."

Hopis notice how Philbert's dolls show his deep commitment to tradition and spirituality. Seeing the way Philbert carves makes the elders happy because not many people carve in this style. They tell Philbert, "This is the way a doll used to look when I was a child, and it brings back my childhood memories."

"I think it's great," Philbert said.

KUWANHEHEY'A
(Fancy Hehey'a).
Barbara Rice collection.

WALTER HOWATO

Walter is the most generous, humble, unassuming man I have ever met, and he entertains guests with story after story from his very interesting life. He was born at Sitsom'ovi on First Mesa, lived most of his life on the reservation, and remembers attending the now-famous Santa Fe Indian School in New Mexico, back in the days when it was more like boot camp. Born in 1921, Walter has been carving for more than sixty years and he has sold all over. However, his work is most easily found at the Heard Museum in Phoenix where he has been selling for over forty years. "I made a lot of old katsina dolls for the Heard Museum. Other Hopis came and told the Heard they shouldn't be hanging there. Why? It's not a ceremonial thing. It's just a *Sa'lako*. Everybody makes *Sa'lako*. I don't make anything ceremonial. So I quit making *Sa'lako* for the museum." Those early katsina dolls sold for ten to fifteen dollars each.

> *"When I first got initiated you just made flat dolls.*
> *A long time ago they were used as a Paaho, to make*
> *a prayer; they were for praying for rain. Then finally*
> *somebody sold one, made two dollars or maybe*
> *fifty cents, and it went on from there."*

On Walter's dining room table sat a fresh pitcher of iced tea and an assortment of his work: four beautiful traditional-style dolls, an incredible contemporary eagle katsina, and a number of paintings. He told me that he likes making the "old katsina dolls" better than making the contemporary. "I'm just not happy making that kind," he said pointing to the contemporary doll, "but it's still hard work making these old katsina dolls, because you have to do them about three times over. You don't paint them just once." His painting style is unusual. He applies the paint and then uses a clean, wet brush to remove a bit here and there. "It's hard. If you use too much water you smear it up." After three or four coats his dolls look as though

OPPOSITE LEFT:
KUWANHEHEY'A
(Fancy Hehey'a).
OPPOSITE CENTER:
SA'LAKWMANA
(no English translation).
OPPOSITE RIGHT:
TANGAQWA
(Rainbow Katsina).
All Barbara Rice collection.

they really are a hundred years old. I assumed he used pigments to paint them, but he caught me off guard when he said that he uses a mixture of poster paints and *tuuma*.

When Walter picks out wood for carving, he is careful to select pieces that fit the old style. "Junk wood, that's the kind I use, cracked and old," he said. This wood makes Walter's dolls look even more ancient. He has used feathers from ducks, parrots, and pheasants, and remembers the old days when you could still use eagle and hawk feathers. Then the federal government passed the Migratory Bird Act and endangered species laws controlling the use of certain feathers. Walter joked about one of the birds they put on this list. "I had a dove feather on this one katsina and the buyer said, 'This is a no-no; this is from a migratory bird.' I laughed and said, 'Migratory nothing, they sit around in my back yard twenty-four hours a day. I guess they don't want to migrate anymore.'"

> *"I guess I've been here too long. I used to see katsinam bring dolls like this for the people. During bean dance, you know. Now it's all gone."*

Most of his life, Walter built highways as a heavy equipment operator, and he even shared a few scary stories about building Glen Canyon Dam. He has accomplished many things and rubbed elbows with many famous and interesting people. Frank Waters, a renowned writer and author of *Book of the Hopi* (Viking Press, 1963), once interviewed Walter as a source for a book he never published. "I met Frank Waters quite some time ago. He bought some katsina dolls from me. One time we were having breakfast in Santa Fe. He started talking about wanting to write another book. He wanted to know about Hopi marriage. I told him the truth about what he wanted to know. And I told him Hopi weddings were just as expensive as a white wedding."

Walter also used to work for Walt Disney in California when he was just starting out. "We did a lot of things. Sometimes I played an Indian at Disneyland, and sometimes I painted and did some interior decorating with my friend R. C. Gorman. R. C. and I painted everything up there."

Nowadays, Walter is concerned with historic preservation and the loss of culture at Hopi. He is worried that the kids don't take enough interest in their culture and religion and that many don't speak Hopi. He feels that many things are not documented and the handful of people who still know certain things are getting older and may not be around much longer. "The coming of the white man, nobody ever told the straight real truth about his coming, how he's going to be, and what he's going to bring. It's what you see outside— pollution and homes. We used to have dirt roads, no bridges out there. People would say, 'Why can't we have that?' The Hopi leaders just said, 'No.' If we build a good road, if we build a railroad, when you get into an argument with your wife she will pack up her stuff, go to the highway and hitchhike somewhere.

"The white man wants to come here and create jobs for Indians and build a little shirt factory. The Hopi leaders say, 'No.' Hopis ask 'Why?' Because when they (Anglos) come to do that, they need a place to live, so they have to build houses here. Then they bring their experts and they need a place to live and soon they'll build more houses, run you out of the reservation. That's what happens. They bring something in and pretty soon there are houses, houses, houses."

Though non-Indians have made mistakes in the past, Walter believes they should still be made welcome at Hopi. He recalls that in the 1960s there were some horrible incidents of theft and vandalism of shrines. These few bad experiences with tourists led to village closures. Walter feels, however, that the Hopi religion is for everyone.

Kwikwilyaqa
(Imitator).
Barbara Rice collection.

> *"I've been to a lot of katsina ceremonies and when the chief speaks, he speaks for every living thing on this Earth, for everyone throughout the world. People should enjoy our prayers. We are dancing; that's how we pray."*

My conversation with Walter was a heartwarming experience. His expert storytelling and great sense of humor made me feel at ease. When it came time to take his picture he stood against the white wall and looked to the side. After I snapped the initial shot he

Sı'ohemiskatsina
(*Zuni Hemis Katsina*).
Barbara Rice collection.

grabbed an old license plate off a table and held it up to his chest as if he was waiting for me to take his mug shot. We couldn't stop laughing. He also did something else so unexpected I was almost speechless. He took the *Kököle* katsina doll (the katsina that recounts Hopi oral history) off the table, handed it to me and said, "Here, this one's for you." This man, whom I had just met, not only treated me like family, but also gave me a wonderful doll to hang in my house.

BARRY WALSH
BUFFALO BARRY'S INDIAN ARTS

BARRY WALSH became interested in the trading business when he bought his first katsina doll in San Diego in 1987. As he read more on katsinam his interest grew and he decided to make a trip to the Hopi Reservation; he's been going ever since. Today, his Worcester, Massachusetts–based company, Buffalo Barry's Indian Arts, doesn't have a store front, but his reputation draws many private collectors from all over the world.

Soon after discovering his interest in Hopi, Barry stumbled upon the traditional-style dolls. He read an article on Manfred Susunkewa and was immediately attracted to the style. He contacted Manfred directly and, in his words, "harassed him" into selling him a few dolls. A relationship developed and Barry has been collecting and selling them ever since. "I think it's the basic justification that comes from the carvers of going back to an expression of spirit and not using artistic tour de force as the priority. I still like contemporary dolls. It's not like I'm a purist. I like all kinds of katsina dolls, but I think the traditional dolls speak to me more often."

Barry has a different view on this style than many of his colleagues. "I view these dolls as artistically distinctive from the traditional-style dolls that were given at the turn of the century. It is a very separate and distinct artistic tradition that, nonetheless, emerged from the dolls that were given to children. Are they similar? Yes, but the eye of the modern traditional-style carver is different. It sees the world differently and executes a different type of physical carving."

In a relatively short period of time Barry has become an authority on katsina dolls and has been asked to write numerous articles on related subjects. One such article, "The Controversial Mass Production of Navajo 'Kachina' Dolls," appeared in *The Indian Trader* (March 1994) regarding imitation katsina dolls made by a small group of Navajos. He infiltrated this Anglo-owned katsina-doll factory as if to do a sincere story about their product. "I discovered they were making these dolls on an assembly line, using power tools. One person would rip them with the power tools, the next one would power sand them, and the next one would paint them with house paint. The very last one, the dresser, would stick on the rabbit fur and sign them as if he had created the whole product." Barry has also written other articles for *The Indian Trader* as well as for *American Indian Art, Santa Fe Monthly,* and the *Haffenreffer Museum Newsletter.* He also curated a long-running exhibit on traditional-style dolls at the Haffenreffer Museum of Anthropology at Brown University.

Wallace Hyeoma

The day we talked, Wallace was carving at his mother's house. Other than the fact that it was made of cinder blocks (fast becoming a traditional building material) the house reminded me of most of my Hopi relatives' homes. It has two rooms: One is for sleeping, and the other is a kitchen/dining area. Modest, yet fully functional living is a common theme of Hopi architecture. The walls were lined with corn husks from the recent harvest, soon to be made into tamales and *sumiviki* (a traditional Hopi sweet). Photos of relatives and art decorated the house and a coal stove in the corner kept us toasty. Through and through a traditional Hopi home; a fitting place for a carver as traditional as Wallace.

Born in Tuba City, Arizona, sixty-five miles from where he now lives in Songòopavi atop Second Mesa. He grew up speaking Hopi and didn't learn English until he started school. That's rare these days, as more and more Hopi kids grow up in front of the television. Wallace voiced his concern about those kids and pointed out that all too often, when older Hopis speak to a child in Hopi, the kid will just stare back in confusion. Wallace says he's lucky because a lot of people his age don't speak Hopi, but he grew up around his grandparents. "That's where I learned a lot of things," he said. "Hopi was all they spoke around me. If it's spoken in the home when kids are babies they'll learn it, they'll speak it, and they won't forget it even if they move away." Wallace and his mother moved to Winslow when he was in the eighth grade. When the new high school opened at Hopi he was already a junior, and his mother decided to move home. Wallace ended up graduating from Hopi High.

> *"I think it's one of the most important things. To be Hopi is to speak the language and to understand it."*

Wallace started carving in the mid-1980s. Today he mostly sells directly to passing tourists from a bench outside the Hopi Cultural Center. Like many carvers, he began carving flat dolls while hanging

OPPOSITE LEFT:
Hilili
(no English translation).
Jonathan S. Day collection.

OPPOSITE CENTER:
So'yok.wùuti
(Orgre Woman).
Quotskuyva collection.

OPPOSITE RIGHT:
Tsa'kwayna Taaha'amu
(no English translation).
Courtesy Tsakurshovi.

around his uncles. Wallace watched his uncles carve and then picked up a knife and started himself. "You're always improving," he said. "You look at your doll and there's something you may not like about it, so the next time you make it you try to correct it. You're just experimenting." Then in the late 1980s, while working at a trading post specializing in traditional-style dolls, he decided to give it a try. "I just like the way they look. They're more simple; it's an old type of carving. It's like the kind that you see in museum collections, and the colors are real earth tones."

> *"Not many carvers do traditional dolls. It's kind of*
> *different than what everyone else is doing, plus it's like*
> *the kind they [katsinam] give away."*

Wallace's carving style employs many uncommon methods. For instance, he doesn't use mineral pigments when he paints, because the pigments get into the bristles and make the tips flare out. To avoid the constant expense of buying new brushes, he uses acrylics. "When they're watered down with a lot of water they come out pastel-looking like the old colors." He also does something none of his peers do. He carves around every detail or color change in the doll before he paints. "I use a lot of water, so it tends to bleed. So I cut in everywhere it's going to be painted. That way the color only bleeds as far as the cut, and it won't bleed into the rest of the colors. I draw it on first and go over it with my knife. It takes a lot of time."

A lot of work and a lot of time have paid off for Wallace. He has figured out what works and people love his art. "I think I do well with my dolls because when I sell a doll I explain it so the buyer understands what I made, how I made it, and the style of carving."

How does he pick what to carve? Sometimes it's what the market demands. "Right now my favorite one is an owl. I don't know what it is with owls, but they're selling for me right now." Sometimes he just carves what he sees. "I like carving the katsinam that I see at dances, but sometimes there are dolls that shouldn't be carved. Sooner or later everybody has to pay a price. I wouldn't really want to carve something I shouldn't and usually my uncles would tell me."

The katsina Wallace is best known for, however, is his rendering of a frog, or *Paakwa*. "My uncle, Roxie Pela, was the first guy I saw carve a frog. I just liked the way they looked, so I started making them and kind of became famous for my frogs. Everyone wants a frog. I've still got a big waiting list. I've only seen the real thing one time in my whole life. The mudheads came and had a gambling game, a guessing game with the village ladies. They had this box covered up and the Hopi ladies had to guess what was in the box. It was one of the longest games. It lasted from about 3:30 in the afternoon until seven or eight at night because nobody could guess what was in that box. One of the ladies finally guessed and as soon as she said

LEFT:
MOSAYURMANA
(Buffalo Maiden).
Sun face detail shown below.

RIGHT:
PAAKWA *(Frog).*
Both Tsakurshovi.

'frog' that frog katsina jumped out of the box. This was probably twenty years ago."

His take on tourists' fascination with Hopi is one shared with others on the mesas. "They read a lot of books about how we're probably one of the few tribes that still have a lot of our culture intact. It kind of pulls people. They want to come out here and find out what we're like and get into the ceremonies. I think it's all the ceremonial stuff that really appeals to people. We're a magnet for people; they want to learn something. However, Hopis are real secretive. We can't talk about everything and we ourselves don't know everything by the time we grow up and die."

"They come out here looking for teepees and Indians with two feathers sticking out of their heads, and that's a big misconception right there."

People also go out to the mesas looking for art. Wallace says he and others carvers never thought of this as art because they use it in their culture. But when the first tourist came by and started buying, that's when people thought of the dolls as art and started making them for sale. "This is my only source of income; this is what I do," Wallace says. "Even if you go out and get a job, you have something to fall back on if you lose your job or get hurt. It's a way of living for a lot of people out here."

Wallace welcomes tourists to visit the reservation and see what it's all about. In fact, if you're buying dolls, he suggests that you visit the Hopi Reservation to make sure you're buying the genuine article. "We don't let anyone out here sell dolls that aren't real, and no two pieces of art are ever the same."

ALSTON AND DEBORAH NEAL

OLD TERRITORIAL SHOP

IN OLD TOWN SCOTTSDALE you'll find a little shop that is jam packed with great art. It's called the Old Territorial Shop and it is the oldest trading post on Main Street in Scottsdale, Arizona. The owners, Alston and Debbie, are more than happy to educate visitors on any or all items in their shop. Native American art is their favorite topic and they have many interesting stories to share. In a town that has so many over-the-top galleries, it's nice to walk into a shop and soak up the old-time trading post feel.

They also sell some of the best traditional-style dolls. "The operative word is 'doll,' not 'sculpture.' How many times have you seen a four-thousand-dollar action doll being given away at a dance? The essence of what we think about is the purity, whether it be jewelry, baskets, pottery, or rugs. It's the traditional, the way things have always been, it's what lasts the longest. When we look back at the 1970s stuff we think, yuck! But when you look at the 1970s traditional stuff, you like it and it's what still sells. That's why we like the traditional-style dolls."

The Neals' vast knowledge of Indian art is amazing. Alston also grew up in the business and is an expert in many fields. Their shop also carries a wide variety of Native American antiquities. These folks have been great about promoting and educating people about this style. "People come in looking for imitation dolls because they can't afford a Hopi doll. Well, a traditional-style Hopi cradle doll costs less than an imitation doll and most importantly, it's real."

RAMSON LOMATEWAMA

Ramson Lomatewama is a multitalented artist from Hotvela. A traditional Hopi, he speaks his native language and participates actively in his religion. At first glance his complexion, his frame, and even his traditional Hopi haircut cries out typical Edward Curtis Indian, though he is anything but stereotypical. His "Don't Worry Be Hopi" T-shirt is the first tip. He is a successful silversmith, glass blower, stained glass artist, master woodworker, poet, and traditional-style doll carver. He lectures and teaches all over the country. He currently resides in Flagstaff, Arizona, and plans to move back to the Hopi Reservation and open a glass blowing studio with his wife and children. We spoke at his studio just outside of Flagstaff. The dirt road approaching the converted garage is a bit hard on the shocks, but people have sacrificed their rental cars for years for the chance to be entertained by this artist.

> *"The money's okay, but that's not the total picture.*
> *It's the spirit of the feelings and the heart that*
> *I put into that work."*

Ramson was born in Victorville, California, in 1953. His father, along with several other men from Hotvela, were working for the Santa Fe Railroad at the time. He was three when his family returned to the Hopi Reservation. His parents separated when he was in second grade, and his mother, seeking work, moved the family to Flagstaff. Even though he lived in the city and attended school full time, Ramson spent almost every weekend at Hopi. The summers were filled with dances and ceremonies, and the rest of the year they would visit family and friends. Ramson feels this may be one of the most important parts of his upbringing. Surrounded by the city Monday through Friday, he still managed a traditional way of life, even if only on the weekends. "I was a weekend warrior," he said as he smiled proudly, put his hands on his waist, and puffed out his chest like a superhero. Ramson enrolled in the pre-med program at Northern

OPPOSITE LEFT:
KOOKOPÖLÖ
(Assassin Fly).
Ramson Lomatewama collection.
OPPOSITE CENTER:
MASAWKATSINA
(no English translation).
Barbara Rice collection.
OPPOSITE RIGHT:
HÒNKATSINA
(Bear Katsina).
Ramson Lomatewama collection.

ÙMTOYNAQA
(no English translation).
Ramson Lomatewama collection.

Arizona University after he graduated from high school but with-drew by the end of his sophomore year. "It wasn't my calling, I guess. I quit school, married, and started a family."

Remarkably, art wasn't his first calling either. To support his family Ramson took jobs ranging from welder to exterminator. In his early twenties he took a job with the tribe and moved back to Hotvela. During that period Ramson received his undergraduate degree from Goddard College, a nontraditional college in Vermont, and that's when he discovered poetry.

When he was twelve Ramson began carving but had never fully pursued it as a career. He had sold a few dolls in the past, but carv-ing would not become prominent in his life for some time. Instead he turned to writing. Over the next few years Ramson published sev-eral collections of poetry, including *Drifting Through Ancestor Dreams* (Entrada Books, 1993) and *Silent Winds: Poetry of One Hopi* (Badger claw Press, 1987). He also traveled to different schools and taught poetry as part of the Heard Museum's artist-in-residence program.

As his writing ability developed, Ramson also discovered new creative endeavors. He started with stained glass containing Hopi themes and eventually moved on to the art of blowing glass. While lecturing at various college campuses he learned more and more about this art form and bartered lecture fees for studio time in the schools' art departments. He then attended the Pilchuck Glass School in Washington state, the most prominent glass school in the country. His work in this medium is on display throughout the Southwest. One day he plans to build a glass studio on the reservation not only to blow glass, but also to teach this art form to Hopi children.

Though Ramson began carving katsina dolls as an income source during the mid-1990s, he remembers selling a doll when he was much younger. It may have been the first doll he carved without the help of a family member. He sold it to a local trader in Flagstaff for five dollars. The buyer asked him to carve out the fingers next time instead of just painting them on. "I guess that's kind of how artists are influenced, especially by those traders and what the art market will demand or what their perception of it is. Obviously, he also wants to earn a living. If he's selling dolls that have carved fingers, he's probably going to tell as many guys as he can to carve those fingers." He took the trader's advice and further refined his style but sold only intermittently until he switched to the traditional style.

> *"I'm trying to express what people were trying to*
> *express a long time ago, before the commercial stuff*
> *started to influence doll carving. I'm making a living.*
> *I'm not anti-commercial; I'm just pro back-to-basics."*

The first time he decided to, as he puts it, "get back to basics" was when he saw Manfred Susunkewa's dolls at a show in Phoenix and had the chance to talk with him about them. "He was just explaining to me what his view of the whole carving thing was and it really hit home. I adopted some of his philosophies and started carving that way."

Ramson is what those in the trading business call a "hard-core" traditional carver. Not only does he make his own paints from native pigments, but he also goes so far as to hand spin his own cotton for attaching feathers. His tools are what a turn-of-the-century carver may have owned. "Most carvers had a pocket knife, a small hand saw, and if you were really lucky, you had a steel rasp." Ramson even sands his dolls with sandstone, and a local plant called *siwi* is used to peg on the ears and mouth. Ramson's dolls are a hit among many tourists, and after seeing his fifteen-minute seminar describing his work, it's no wonder that he is successful.

> *"People are relying on a romantic, stereotypical view of*
> *Indians. They think we're all spiritual, in tune with the*
> *earth, and all that stuff. It's some kind of Indian, but*
> *it's not an Indian of reality."*

Although it seems the charmed life of an artist and scholar, Ramson's life, as with anyone's, has had its ups and downs. Not only did he lose a father and two brothers to alcoholism, but he also confronted alcohol. "I drank, but one day you just wake up and you're tired of it." Giving up that lifestyle wasn't easy, but he had help. "One of the things that helped me down that path was getting reinvolved with ceremony and ritual." By the time he was diagnosed

SA'LAKWMANA
(Sa'lako Maiden).
Ramson Lomatewama collection.

with diabetes he was alcohol-free, and this new development gave him an extra incentive to stay that way. Taking better care of oneself isn't easy, but when faced with a life-threatening illness, people learn to change. After years of insulin dependence, Ramson decided he wasn't going to be a diabetic anymore. He told himself, "I'm not going to be sick anymore," and repeated this every day for years. He eventually stopped taking his daily injections and remains insulin-free to this day. "I just watch what I eat and I exercise."

BARBARA RICE
COLLECTOR

PENNSYLVANIA-BASED Barbara Rice owns more than 200 traditional-style dolls—the world's largest collection—and many of her dolls were photographed for this book. She is what I like to call a "convert," meaning she first began collecting contemporary katsina dolls. "I was walking along Canyon Road in Santa Fe and came across a shop and saw the action-style katsina dolls for the first time. I was immediately attracted to them and bought my first doll there. The following year I took a trip to Arizona and went up to the Hopi Reservation. I first saw the traditional style there. I thought they were much more mysterious and interesting, particularly because they were not as realistic as the action dolls. They were more minimal in style and captured for me an essence that was more meaningful, artistically speaking."

Today all she collects are the traditional dolls. She makes trips to Arizona often and takes advantage of mail order. Her advice for people considering collecting: "Become familiar with a range of different artists by visiting shops both on and off the reservation. Pick up a book or two on the meanings of these dolls in Hopi religion and learn about their function as well as some information about how the carving and painting is done."

CLIFFTON LOMAYAKTEWA

I was house-sitting for my parents on Second Mesa the day I ran into Clifffton. He came over to their shop, Tsakurshovi, (page 27) to sell some dolls. He had about six or seven, each of them neatly wrapped in a paper towel and carefully arranged in a cardboard box.

Clifffton was born at Orayvi in the village proper. I've overheard some locals joke, "Now that's a real Hopi, actually born in the vil'." That day his father was busy working the family's cornfield when Clifffton's mother gave birth alone in their little sandstone home. When his father returned from farming, they took Clifffton to the hospital at Keams Canyon just to make sure everything was okay.

While Clifffton was growing up, his parents worked for the Fred Harvey Company at the Grand Canyon during the tourist season. Clifffton stayed with his grandparents and attributes much of his knowledge to them, along with other Hopi elders.

> *"I get a lot of inspiration from the old folks. They tell me just to keep it up. Keep it up, don't lose it, because that's one of the first things they learned. Those old-style dolls and pigments."*

Clifffton attended high school at the Phoenix Indian School, which has since closed. Other educational options were available, but Clifffton wanted to leave the reservation and experience something different. After graduating he attended construction school with the hopes of getting a good job in the booming Phoenix housing market. He had a great job lined up, but his first child was on the way so he decided to move back to Hopi. He took up fire-fighting and now travels the country as the sqaud leader of the Hopi Hot Shots, an all-Hopi wildland firefighting crew. He runs three miles a day to stay in shape.

Now living below First Mesa with his wife in a nice mobile home. Clifffton works in his nearby cornfield and lives the life of a traditional

OPPOSITE LEFT:
SO'YOK.WÙUTI
(Ogre Woman).
Jonathan S. Day collection.
OPPOSITE CENTER:
ÙMTOYNAQA
(no English translation).
Barbara Rice collection.
OPPOSITE RIGHT:
PAAKWA (FROG).
Jonathan S. Day collection.

MONGKATSINA
(no English translation).
Barbara Rice collection.

Hopi, but he still reminisces about his younger years in Orayvi and regrets some of the changes that have taken place.

"It's getting too modern out here. Now there's not even a donkey to ride. There also used to be pigs and sheep. When I was a kid we used to go to the 'ass house' and ride the donkeys around. My grandfather still has his wagon at the village. He used to take it out to the field fifty miles south of Orayvi. It would take a whole day to get there and a whole day back." He also fears he is forgetting his language. He's fluent in Hopi, but rarely has the opportunity to speak it. "Nobody at First Mesa really talks Hopi; I'm kind of losing it. Maybe I need to move back home [Orayvi]."

"I like the traditional style because it brings back
a lot of memories from a long time ago."

First Mesa is where Cliffton first learned about the traditional style. After he was married he moved to Polacca but didn't know anyone there. At first he would sit around his mother-in-law's house and carve contemporary-style dolls. Eventually he made some friends, and one was Manuel Denet Chavarria, Jr. (page 22).

"One day I went down to Manuel's house and he was there carving these traditional-style dolls," Cliffton said. "He asked me to try it out, so I did. He's the one that got me back into this old style."

Cliffton had been carving in the contemporary style, but found the traditional style more rewarding and he's been carving them that way ever since. He carved contemporary for about four to five years, and was doing pretty well, but he couldn't get into the details of the hands. That's the part that got me," he said. Now Cliffton carves a large selection of both Third Mesa and First Mesa katsinam. Which katsinam he carves is an unconscious decision. "I just relax and let my hands do the work. If I'm into it, it comes out real quick. If not, I'll just put it down and try something else."

Cliffton doesn't have to try to make his dolls stand out. He uses many of the same pigments that other carvers use, but the way he mixes them makes the colors stands out. He adds clear acrylic to his black, but the rest of his palette is pigment and water. He likes the pigments so much that he will sometimes not sell a doll and instead give it to the elements. "I like to put them out in the rain and get them all dirty and stuff. Just make a doll and set it outside and let it pour down." The resulting appearance reminds him again of their true purpose: bringers of life and rain.

> *"Some people tell me to mix [my pigments] all up so they won't rub off, but I like it that way. That's how they're supposed to be. That's how we made them a long time ago."*

KOONAKATSINA
(Squirrel Katsina).
Barbara Rice collection.

When he's not carving, Cliffton is fighting forest fires. You can often find his work in The Monongya Gallery on Third Mesa, Tsakurshovi (page 27), and Winter Sun (page 87), even during the fire season, and during his time off he sells directly to tourists in the village. Cliffton also enjoys giving dolls away. "Last year I made some small ones and gave them away to a few of the village elders. I like to do that sometimes because it will help me out. Not just selling them all the time, but also giving them away." Cliffton is very respectful of his elders. He credits them with helping him succeed and enjoys their reaction to his work. "A lot of old folks I show them to like them because they bring back a lot of memories of what they received when they were small."

VERNON MANSFIELD

Born and raised on the Hopi Reservation at Songòopavi, Vernon has worked at various jobs over the years. He held a retail position at the Watchtower at the Grand Canyon for a while and thinned trees for the U.S. Forest Service in Happy Jack, Arizona. Most of his life, however, has been spent as an artist, rancher, and farmer. Whether silversmithing, carving, branding, or planting, Vernon is always busy. He is a shy and modest artist, but I was made welcome in his home and his smile and laughter set me at ease right away.

We sat in his work area, a living room–sized space sparsely decorated with an enormous desk in front of a window that looked out on Songòopavi village. Vernon was working on an order for Tsakurshovi (page 27) and was at the painting stage on about five dolls. Vernon has been carving the traditional style for sale since the early 1980s and his style is easily recognizable from other carvers by his painting. So I asked him what was in those twenty or so little jars that dotted his desktop, and he told me it was just tempera paint, the kind people used until someone invented latex acrylics. This surprised me. Vernon is about as traditional as they come so I assumed he would use pigments. He said in the old days he did, but switched to avoid being confused with other carvers. "Pigments are hard to make," he said. "Tempera is just easier."

Vernon opened a drawer in his desk and began pulling out various Tupperware containers filled with his old pigment paints. Over the course of about an hour I came to realize that this desk had about everything you could imagine in it. Every time I commented on something, he would open a new drawer and pull out photos or letters and even his silverwork and cut stones. The answer to any question I had was somewhere in that desk. As we talked about colors he shared with me his knowledge of plants.

OPPOSITE LEFT:
KOONINKATSINA
(Supai Katsina).
OPPOSITE CENTER:
LÖLÖQUANGW PAVOKA
(Snake Guard).
OPPOSITE RIGHT:
KOO' ÀAKATSINA
(no English translation).
All Tsakurshovi.

"My grandfather taught me how to make
colors from plants."

The yellow flowers from *siwi,* a Hopi plant often used to peg on
the ears and mouths of katsina dolls, is used to make a bright yellow.
There is also a clay found in a nearby spring that can be used to make
a mustard yellow. The flowers of a local mint sage are boiled to make
purple, and the leaves are used as a spice. This is just a short list of
Vernon's vast knowledge of the old ways. One of the older traditional-
style carvers, he is also one of the few who really remembers what
the Hopi Reservation was like in the old days. Vernon carves what he
likes and his choices are random, but they always reflect his memories, and he often depicts rare katsinam that are no longer seen at
most villages. As we looked at some photos of his previous work, he
pointed at one. "I saw that one when I was a kid," he said. "A lot of
them don't come around anymore."

He will carve just about anything you ask him to unless it is
against the rules of the Hopi religion. He also enjoys carving the
action dolls and continues to carve them today.

No matter what style he carves Vernon never has a problem selling, and he only sells through galleries these days. He gave up mar-
keting them on his own many years ago for the simple reason that
he was burned one too many times. Someone would give him a
deposit and take the doll, promising to send the rest upon returning
home. The check would never come.

Katsina dolls aren't Vernon's only art form. He also learned how
to silversmith at the Hopi Silver Cooperative Guild in 1956. From its
early days through its heyday as the place to buy Hopi art, Vernon
was an integral part of that institution. He showed me some of his
work, and the simple elegance and traditional design impressed me.
"I'm not doing silver now because my kids borrowed all my tools
and my torches and I never got them back."

Vernon has two cornfields and owns a herd of cattle, and even
at sixty-nine he continues to brand them with the help of his oldest
son. In 1969 he started with eight head and his herd is now eighty
strong. As a gift he has given each of his children ten head of cattle

to start their own herds with the hope that it will help provide them with some future security. He also counts on his livestock to help him out when he's in a pinch. He will often trade cows for the sheep he needs for a wedding or dance and, if the family is ever low on cash, they can always sell a cow to get by.

When Vernon is not tending his field or his livestock you may find him making his dolls and his wife weaving baskets in their home in Songòopavi. Vernon's dolls are some of the best on the market, and the bright colors seem to reflect the true use of the dolls. After all, they are for children, and children like bright colors. Demand is so high for his work that he can hardly keep up. Tsakurshovi (page 27) is the only store Vernon sells to.

LEFT:
TASAP MANA
(Navajo Maiden).
RIGHT:
MANANG.YAKATSINA
(Blue-collared Lizard).
Both Tsakurshovi.

LARRY MELENDEZ

I first met Larry when I started managing Winter Sun Trading Company in Flagstaff (page 87). He came in with his brother, Manuel Denet Chavarria, Jr., (page 22) when he was just starting out with the traditional style. He had a Tewa clown and I bought it—personally, not for resale—for fifty dollars. I was thrilled with it, and it became the first doll in my collection. Today, I could never buy one like it that inexpensively, but this was the early 1990s and the market was just opening up for this style. I had kind of a running deal with Larry as well as several other carvers: They would sell me dolls for my personal collection at a serious discount on the condition that I would never re-sell them. The next two dolls I bought were also Larry's, and to this day his dolls are some of the best in my collection.

Larry was eighteen when his brother began teaching him how to carve. He started with one or two full-figured contemporary dolls, and from there he mostly carved sculptures—and not very many at that. "I didn't do it that much," he said. "They were few and far between." Manuel soon passed on his knowledge of the traditional style and that's when Larry really started getting into the business.

> *"Like a lot of other kids out there, you're influenced by everybody around you who carves the same thing, contemporary or traditional."*

Today, all of Larry's income comes from carving, but this wasn't always so. Larry was born in Phoenix and raised Catholic. His mother is Hopi and he went to the reservation for dances, but he didn't become involved in ceremonies until he was eighteen. "That was another half of my life I had to seek out. I wasn't around it that much." By that time in his life he had a middle management job and was considering a transfer to Orlando, Florida. As his trips to the reservation became more frequent, so did his desire to stay. "I was in the rat race for a while, but Rez life wasn't as hectic as being in the city. Each and every time I'm up on the mesa, I look off the

OPPOSITE LEFT:
MAAHUKATSINA
(Cicada Katsina).
Jonathan S. Day collection.
OPPOSITE CENTER:
HOOTE
(no English translation).
Jonathan S. Day collection.
OPPOSITE RIGHT:
SI'OHOOTE
(Zunit Hoote).
Barbara Rice collection.

MOMOKATSINA *(Bee).*
Honeycomb detail shown below.
Barbara Rice collection.

edge and I'm like, 'Wow!' It probably added forty to fifty years to my life. I'm not so stressed."

That forty to fifty years he's talking about is no joke. Larry told me he believes his culture and the art of carving saved his life or at least kept him out of jail. "When I lived in south Phoenix, there were twenty to thirty different ways to get paid, none of them legal. I was in a gang and out of about seven close friends, four of us are still living and out of those, half are in prison. Once you're in something like that you're always in. I'm still considered a part of it. But it was a part of me developing into the person I am. There is a lot of street knowledge that went with that. There are a lot of things books can't teach you, but I wouldn't recommend that path to anyone." Larry believes that his experiences on the streets, good or bad, can only be looked at positively. If not for those experiences, he may never have sought out the Hopi half of his culture. All those things led him to the life he now lives.

His culture and his art are very important to him, and not simply because art provides a financial benefit. "I believe [the katsinam] are really teaching tools for kids. Each and every one of them has something that they give us to make our full-life cycle. Katsinam are seasonal, but they leave examples for us to follow throughout the year. That's what I believe we are supposed to do."

"There are some things that happen in Hopi that you just can't explain in English."

Carving is an emotional release for Larry. Like a proud father seeing his newborn child for the first time, he loves the finished product. The enjoyment of looking at his dolls hanging on a wall seems to be Larry's greatest reward. "I like the way they come out when they're finished. Each time you mix your paints it's something different. It's an expression through color tones." He says he can even look at older dolls and know, just from the paints, when he carved them and what was happening in his life at the time.

He decides what to carve by the wood he has on hand. Sometimes it takes him a while to fill an order because he's waiting for the right piece of wood. "You start out with a piece of wood, and you sometimes see it already. You look at the way it is and you're like, 'Oh, I know what to do with this!' I can just see what it is; it's looking back at me."

> *"Sometimes wood has certain shapes or certain bends that you use for certain dolls."*

Today, Larry produces some of the best dolls around. "It took me a couple of years to become consistent. I like doing it. It's a challenge. It's not as easy as everybody thinks. Gathering materials is really hard." Many of the materials can only be traded for with other tribes. Some may only be available on the Hopi Reservation. "To carve old style dolls you need organic materials. You can't just walk into Kmart and buy parrot feathers, or horsehair, or *tuuma.*"

TUSKYAPKATSINA
(Crazy Rattle Katsina).
Winter Sun Trading Company.

Larry was a young adult when he sold his first dolls to the Heard Museum in Phoenix. "It was really hard to sell them at first. People had to be reeducated about what they were buying because they were so used to the contemporary dolls. It's easier to sell now." Larry lives on and off the reservation, but, if he's there, you can still find him selling on First Mesa. He and his friends hang out, carve, and chat with the tourists.

Right now he's spending a lot of time in Flagstaff, but still sells throughout Arizona. Even though this style has really caught the public's eye and demand is up, Larry is still picky about who he sells to. "I look for authenticity in the shops I sell to. I will walk in and if it's full of imitation dolls, I'll just turn around and not even bother. It's bad enough that we're outnumbered by people imitating Hopi art. I don't want to contribute to that. That's why I look for authenticity, that what that shop sells is real, and I stick with those shops. They're more educated about what they're selling and they care more about what they're selling."

Larry sometimes works part time at the Winter Sun Trading Company (page 87). His big smile, deep laugh, and natural ability to interact with people makes for a fun shopping experience. You might even be lucky enough catch him carving on the job.

Tay Polequaptewa

Tay began carving traditional-style dolls in the early 1990s, and he's been carving sculptures a few years longer. When his mother worked at Keams Canyon, she would take his sculptures to work with her and sell them to a variety of people. Tay lived in Songòopavi and did what most Hopi men his age did: he carved. Spending time with Philbert Honanie (page 36), Bertram Tsavadawa (page 98), and Wallace Hyeoma (page 46) eventually rubbed off on him. "I just hung out with my buddies and we all just carved," he said. "We'd stay at somebody's *piiki* house [where Hopi women make *piiki*, or ceremonial bread] and we all learned from each other. You know, one of the older guys would be there, doing fine work, and we were just starting out." He started carving more of the traditional style and found he really enjoyed the process. "A lot of people do the contemporary style already, the action dolls. They use a Dremel and all those machines, and I prefer using a knife and simple tools. It's fun to make them. I like putting all the feathers on there and making them look how I've seen them."

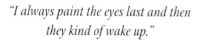

*"I always paint the eyes last and then
they kind of wake up."*

In those days, Tay was still singing with a powwow group called Sacred Star. They won many awards on the powwow circuit for their original songs with Hopi lyrics, and even recorded an album. They found time to practice while they worked. "We were all singing together, and so we'd carry all of our wood somewhere and carve and make songs." Eventually, as Tay put it, "They all grew up and started having kids, and so we stopped touring. We all still sing, though."

That early, detailed work has led to a very different traditional style. If you look closely at Tay's dolls you'll notice his attention to detail, not just in the accessories but in his painting as well. Tay's dolls are almost a hybrid of the two styles: Taking the best from the contemporary dolls and applying it to the traditional dolls makes

OPPOSITE LEFT:
Putskòomotaqa
(Scorpion).
Winter Sun Trading Company.

OPPOSITE CENTER:
Tsaaveyo
(no English translation).
Jonathan S. Day collection.

OPPOSITE RIGHT:
Nuvaktsimana
(Snow Maiden).
Winter Sun Trading Company.

for an eye-catching, unique appearance. For Tay, carving is a process that shouldn't be rushed. "Since it's not my only source of income I can take my time on them. It takes me a while to put the feathers and all the other stuff on. I like doing the extras; it makes me feel better."

"Even the older guys tell us in the kiva, 'It's neat how you young kids woke this back up.' Now at dances you'll see a lot of these kinds of dolls."

Though he enjoys the natural colors, Tay admits it's probably the most time-consuming part of the process. "It took me a while to learn. I just keep mixing them and wait for the doll to dry. Then I rub my hand on it and see if it rubs off. If it doesn't, then it's done." Tay mixes more *tuuma* with pigment into his paint, which means that his paint rubs off less. "It takes me about a week to come up with all the colors. It takes me a whole day to just make red, blue, yellow, and black—just the major ones."

Tay feels the simplicity and natural materials are the main attraction for katsina doll collectors. "I think a lot of the appeal has to do with the colors, plus the dolls are more natural. Hopi never had any kind of special tools or stains. You would hunt with a slingshot, go kill your birds, and use the feathers to dress up your dolls with. You'd take natural leather and the shells that you traded for and use them on your doll. They used to use nails instead of glue and all the feathers were tied on."

Full participation in Hopi cultural life may be Tay's most important goal. "We're not supposed to be lazy when it comes to ceremonies. We put everything else aside. There might be a big powwow somewhere, but if we have a ceremony going on at home we'll put that powwow aside because this is our way of life; it should come first." That dedication includes teaching the next generation of Hopis about their heritage. "That's one of the reasons songs are important. If a child can learn a song they can say those words. That's one way to teach children." This cultural perseverance is also what draws non-Indians to the reservation. "We still hold all of our ceremonies, the dances that we do. There are other Native Americans who have forgotten their own ceremonies."

KOYAALA
(Tewa Clown).
Detail shown below holding
piiki and watermelon.
Jonathon S. Day collection.

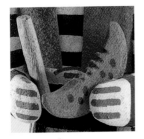

Tay was born and raised on the Hopi Reservation and attended
Sherman Indian School in Riverside, California. He played football
and basketball and won many awards for his academics and athlet-
ics. He is still an avid sports fan and enjoys basketball with the rest
of his friends at Hopi. After high school he graduated from the
Scottsdale Culinary Institute and managed a restaurant on the reservation. Five years later, he began looking for something new. He
moved to Flagstaff and started working for a construction company.
The construction work pays more, and this allows him to carve more
as a hobby than as a necessity, and to continue in this tradition.

WUYAQTAYWA
(Broad Face).
Winter Sun Trading Company.

FRED ROSS

I noticed Fred's truck parked at his house as I drove by, so I decided
to drop in. Normally he would have been at his construction job, but
today the winds were too deadly. It took a while, but I finally managed to get out of my truck. The eighty-mile-an-hour gusts nearly
ripped my door off. This was the biggest sandstorm I'd ever experi-
enced, and I would be cleaning sand out of my teeth and ears for
days. All the roads to and from Hopi were closed and even a good
chunk of I-40 was shut down. Fred had been busy cleaning all day,
thanks to the wind, and happened to have time to talk.

Fred began carving in high school soon after he returned to
Hopi from South Dakota. Fred's father is Sioux, his mother, Hopi.
She is Butterfly Clan from Sitsom'ovi on First Mesa, but worked for
the government in South Dakota during Fred's early childhood.
While she worked they lived in Aberdeen, South Dakota, and spent
the remaining time at Hopi.

On the Sioux side his grandmother, Agnes Ross, is the oldest
matriarch of their band and has an honorary doctoral degree to
boot. She and her son have published many books on the Sioux culture and related topics. Though Fred doesn't know as much as he'd
like to about the Sioux culture, he is proud of his family and his
background.

OPPOSITE LEFT:
PIKSONA *(Piiki Eater).*
Jonathan S. Day collection.
OPPOSITE CENTER:
MORIVOSI *(Bean).*
Barbara Rice collection.
OPPOSITE RIGHT:
HURUNGWÙUTI
(Cold Bringing Woman).
Barbara Rice collection.

In 1985 his mother decided to move back to Polacca, Arizona,
where she grew up. Fred had previously spent a few years living with
his Hopi grandparents and quickly became immersed in the Hopi
culture. By his senior year he began carving traditional-style dolls,
partially as a way to buy gasoline to ride his cousin's all-terrain vehi-
cle. "I went over to Manual's [Denet Chavarria, Jr.] (page 22) one
day, and he and Larry [Melendez] (page 66) showed me how to
carve and sand and how to mix the paint and do the feather work. It
just went from there."

When Fred first started carving he would often look through
books for ideas. Soon he was expanding and producing a variety of
dolls. These days his katsina favorite to carve is a *Hemis.* This is a

katsina that comes during the summer gift-giving ceremony. For that reason, on rare occasions, he carves several miniature gifts and ties them in the dolls' hands. Tiny flat dolls, rattles, and bows sometimes adorn his *Hemis,* better expressing one of the true purposes of katsinam.

> *"The traditional style was the first form of katsina doll that came out. It wasn't until later that people started asking you to carve the fingers and get into more detail."*

Painting with a combination of pigments and acrylics, Fred's yellows and whites are all-natural, but his other colors are a mix. One unique thing about his work is his choice for the blue—real dark, almost navy. He feels this sets him apart from other carvers. "Nobody does that color blue. For now, that's mine. You can tell that's my blue; everybody else uses turquoise." Fred said that in the old days the colors weren't so bright, and this is what he's trying to capture—the colors of the katsina.

This color alone is almost enough to identify Fred's dolls, but he does sign the feet FJR and, for added protection, hides his clan mark or FJR somewhere on the doll. "A lot of people are roughing up dolls and claiming that they're from the nineteenth century, so I can look at it and say 'Hey, this is my doll! That's my little butterfly that I stashed, that they thought was part of the pattern of the kilt or something. Just precautions." It turns out that his cautious approach is justified because one of his friends, recently found a doll in a New Mexico shop that was supposedly from the turn of the century. However, his friend pulled it down and realized that not only was the doll less than five years old, but he also carved it. It was merely roughed up and antiqued. The shop owners were just as shocked as Fred's friend and quickly removed the piece.

TAAHA
(Uncle).
Barbara Rice collection.

*"The carving deals with the inner self sometimes,
at least for me. Sometimes you get in those moods
and you just want to carve something new
and real fancy."*

Fred now lives in Kiqötsmovi with his wife, Susan, and their son Tyson. They are contemplating moving to a city for a few years so Susan can earn her teaching certificate. Fred is planning to work a full-time job and carve part time, but admits that he'll really miss the reservation. He likes the wide-open spaces and peace and quiet, and figures this is part of many non-Indian's attraction to Hopi as well. "Tourists come out here and see the stars, and it's not rushed like the city." To those that have never been exposed to it, the culture also has a great allure. "We haven't been moved. I mean, we did our migrations and then we came back. We haven't been kicked off our own reservation or anything like that, and we're still teaching children from birth."

It's this culture that Fred sometimes feels is being lost in the younger generation. "Kids watch videos and they want to jump on a bandwagon and forget who they really are." Fred wishes they had taught the Hopi language in schools when he was growing up. He does speak some Hopi, but admits he would be better at speaking it if he had been given the opportunity to learn more in school without worrying about being teased for mispronouncing something.

Fred sells most of his katsina dolls through a few galleries in Phoenix and Flagstaff, but you may also catch him selling on the reservation. He does the Winter Sun (page 87) show in Flagstaff every summer, but he wouldn't mind participating in other shows. Fred says that he's not really a people person and he feels uncomfortable talking about his work. So he just lets the shops deal with it, but he will talk to the buyers when he's there. Fred is quiet by nature, but he was being modest about his communication skills. He had no problem giving me his take on the traditional style or sharing his feelings about Hopi.

Qööqöqlö
*(no English translation).
Detail below—holding flat doll,
rabbit stick, rattle and lightning
stick; all presents for children.
Barbara Rice collection.*

FERRIS SATALA

Ferris "Spike" Satala is a carver from Songòopavi on Second Mesa. When I arrived at his mother's house he was busy carving and making paint. In an old coffee can he was boiling a plant called *siita* along with wool to make the base he uses for red. He told me that this plant was also good for colds and congestion. I had a cold, and he just happened to have a separate pot brewing of the tea. I had a few cups; it was pretty tasty stuff and it did clear my head.

He began carving the traditional dolls in the mid-1990s, but his style has really only been defined in the last few years. Initially, he struggled with the more common belly-acher style before finding what worked for him. He told me he was inspired by Alph Secakuku's book *Following the Sun and Moon* (Northland Publishing, 1995), which has a lot of pictures of older dolls, and he remembers seeing a really old book about dolls long ago.

> *"My first doll looked like an alien. We were looking
> at it and passing it around and we were
> all laughing at it."*

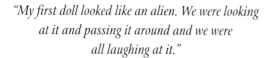

Spike is one of the most unique carvers I've seen in everything from the way he makes his paint to the body form. Like a lot of other carvers he started out with the contemporary style and sold his first two dolls, a *Wupamo* and a racer katsina, to the Hopi Cultural Center Museum when he was in the eighth grade. Spike and three friends took the money next door to the restaurant, ate, and went home empty-handed. Eventually, he gave up the contemporary-style carvings. "They just weren't selling. I wasn't getting what I felt it was worth. There are a few shops that are fair; they make a percentage and that's business." After he gave up carving the contemporary style he did odd jobs around the village until a friend made him a proposition. "Philbert [Honanie] (page 36) said, 'Do some old-style. I'll teach you.'"

Philbert started him painting first. He'd get a big order and he'd ask Spike to help him paint his carvings. Spike started with blue,

OPPOSITE LEFT:
WUPAMO'KATSINA
(Long-billed Katsina).
OPPOSITE CENTER:
KOYAALA *(Tewa Clown).*
OPPOSITE RIGHT:
WAKASKATSINA *(Cow).*
All Barbara Rice collection.

yellow, and finally red. After a while Philbert told him to try the black, which is used for most of the details, and then he told him to try it on his own, so he did. It was hard at first, but Spike liked it. "I'm glad Philbert taught me," he said, "because he taught me the 'one-stroke' method. Instead of trying to make the lines all perfect and uniform, it's just one stroke of my brush. When I looked at my grandfather's dolls, that's how it was, even the eyes, just one stroke."

When I asked why he liked carving the old style he said he liked the feathers and mixing the colors. The switch from the contemporary to traditional was not only enjoyment but necessity. Arthritis was beginning to set in, creating the fine detail of the contemporary dolls was more difficult to do.

The style was taking off and so was his popularity. He thinks that people like the old-style dolls because everything on them is natural. He talked about using modern tools on dolls—the Dremel and wood-burner—and how, if you use them, they were no longer handmade because a machine touched them. "You're not supposed to burn *paako* (cottonwood root)," he said. "That's one reason I got away from con-temporary carving. You're burning your children up. One time I carved a feather on one (a special feather that only the real katsinam have) and my uncle got mad at me and said, 'Don't do that.' It's just supposed to be a doll, not the real thing."

> *"They say all this stuff at Hopi has a whip, and that*
> *whip will come back at you if you disrespect it. So I try*
> *to stay within the boundaries."*

Spike doesn't use much of the standard mineral pigments; he makes his paint from a variety of things. His black, for example, is coffee, soot, and sugar. He exercises by walking and he uses these walks to collect pigments. Rather than buy or trade for his colors Spike collects colored rocks and grinds them into pigments by hand. Using a hammer he smashes the rocks and sifts out the color in a tutsia (yucca sifter basket). The yellow is clay that he finds. He enjoys using mineral pigments, but he doesn't use what the katsinam use for paint. My girlfriend's grandfather taught me about respect and why we have to be respectful, and so I won't carve certain katsinam."

*"I appreciate art and when I carve I try to make it a
piece of art and not just a craft. I try to put
as much as I can into it."*

Most carvers use some clear acrylic medium to prevent the
paint from rubbing off in your hands, but Ferris doesn't. "When I
used to sell on my own," he said, "someone would ask me, 'Is it all-
natural?' and I got a guilty conscience when I'd lie and say, 'Yeah,'
and there was really some clear acrylic in there. "So I stopped."
These dolls will absorb water and the paint runs. Some neighbors
purchased a doll, which was later rained on, and now they like it
even more. The colors all bled into each other and they said, 'You
should come check out your doll. It looks cool.' They appreciate
them more if it rains on them."

Born at the hospital in Keams Canyon, Spike lived briefly in
California before his mother brought him back to the reservation
when he was three. "Dad drank a lot and I guess my mom just
got tired of it, so we moved back here and settled in
Polacca." His father followed soon after, but his parents divorced by the time Spike reached high
school. "My father taught me a lot. He taught me
how to carve and everything, but he just couldn't
quit drinking."

Spike went to high school in Winslow and
lived in the dorms. "The school was in the top 10
percent in the country, academically," he said.
Spike also chose Winslow because his family did-
n't want him to be too far away. His grandmother
wanted him to come home for ceremonies and
made him go to all the dances. Though his background sounds fairly traditional, he didn't start
speaking Hopi until later in life.

"Hopi should be our first language. I didn't speak
good Hopi until I was twenty-seven. In high school people
used to make fun of me. When it's difficult to speak the language and people make fun of you, you're like, 'Screw this, I
don't want to come back here!' and that's the way I felt. They

Wuyaqtaywa
(Broad Face).
Barbara Rice collection.

SUYANG'EVU
(Left-handed Katsina).
Detail below—quiver full of arrows
with a rabbit stick attached.
Barbara Rice collection.

wouldn't correct me, teach me, or tell me what that word meant. So I quit trying." After high school Spike returned to California where he remained for the next ten years. Then, when he moved back, he would go to Polacca and the older men who knew him when he was a baby told him, "Learn it." They would talk to him in Hopi and he could understand it, but he couldn't speak it. But he learned. Pretty soon they would speak Hopi to him, tell him to speak Hopi back, and, finally, he was speaking it.

Spike's brother, Larry, was a contemporary-style carver who made four or five traditional-style dolls before he died in a car accident in the late 1990s. Spike still has several contemporary dolls that were left unfinished by his late brother.

I also asked Spike if he knew where any of his brother's finished traditional-style dolls were. Out of the four or five dolls that Larry made in this style, Spike only knew the whereabouts of one. So I told him that I owned one of Larry's dolls and thought to myself, "Why do I need this doll? It's a great doll, but even Larry's own mother doesn't have one." Now she does.

Larry Satala,
QööQööQLö
(no English translation).
Satala collection.

Phyllis Hogan
Winter Sun Trading Company

PHYLLIS HOGAN is an Indian trader and ethnobotanist, and her shop in Flagstaff carries a selection of the finest Native American art as well as hundreds of traditional herbs, spices, and teas. She has studied with countless native herbalists and is also one of the most knowledgeable people in the Indian art business. The unique combination of herbs and art has made her store, in business since 1976, a huge success.

In 1991, Phyllis began carrying the traditional-style dolls. "I like the traditional style," she says. "It seems more organic. It's not as sculpted or refined as the contemporary and it has an ancient feeling to it." This love of the style made converting customers a fun challenge. She started out with three or four dolls, and now has over a hundred dolls available at any given time. "At first, people didn't really know what to think of them and we had to explain Hopi [the tribe and the religion] to people. Now the traditional-style dolls are very easy to sell because they're very affordable and the customers like the fact that you can hang them on the wall." By educating the public she has really opened up the off-reservation market for this art form.

Every Fourth of July weekend Phyllis holds an exhibition for the traditional-style carvers. She often stocks up on interesting dolls months in advance and brings them out for sale this one weekend every year. Many collectors fly in for the show because it's an excellent opportunity to see the carvers demonstrate and to interact with them in a way not often available during a chance meeting.

JEROLD SEKLETSTEWA

The road to Jerold's house, though paved, has some of the largest speed bumps I've ever seen. However, the pavement ends abruptly and a dirt driveway leads to his house. Outside, a dog was wandering near an old steel clothesline. The dog was on a chain that didn't seem to be attached to anything. He just dragged it around with him wherever he went. Jerold and his wife live in a modern house decorated in the traditional Hopi fashion, with a lot of great art and a great stereo.

When he was a baby, his family moved to Texas. They had packed up the car and set out for Florida, where Jerold's dad had a job waiting. However, the car decided to go no farther than Texas, and that's where they settled. They found temporary residence in the Dallas projects, but moved into a house when his father found permanent work. Jerold called Dallas home and though his family's vacations were spent on the reservation, he always wanted to get back to Texas and see his friends. Jerold was fourteen when his family moved back to Mùnqapi to take care of his grandparents.

After returning from Dallas, Jerold spoke more Spanish than Hopi and, for a long time, he spoke with a Texas accent, which was a double-edged sword. On the one hand, all the girls loved it and were constantly asking him and his brothers to talk, but this also made all the boys jealous, and they responded to Jerold and his brothers with Hopi insults. Eventually, he picked up Hopi and Navajo and forgot his Spanish altogether, but Jerold still isn't fluent in his own language. He understands it, but he has some trouble speaking it. He regrets that his parents didn't teach him more.

Jerold didn't know much about Hopi traditions or art, either. His first taste of art was in junior high, when he began drawing, and later he tried watercolor painting and pottery. He sold some of his work at the Museum of Northern Arizona and even won an award at the Heard Museum in Phoenix. In high school, Jerold's friends were getting into carving and taught him how. At first, he only carved small representations of katsina heads. He wasn't initiated yet, so his mother

OPPOSITE LEFT:
WUPAMO'KATSINA
(Long-billed Katsina).
Winter Sun Trading Company.
OPPOSITE CENTER:
MONGWA
(Great Horned Owl).
Winter Sun Trading Company.
OPPOSITE RIGHT:
NNGAYAYATAQA
(Swaying Man).
Sekletstewa collection.

wouldn't allow him to carve full-sized dolls. He sold the katsina heads to a local truck stop. "They weren't that great," he said, "but I was making two dollars apiece for them just to get candy or balloons or whatever." Gradually, he progressed to the full-sized contemporary dolls, which he sold for fifty dollars at a now-defunct trading post in Flagstaff, and he continued to do well with them throughout Arizona. Jerold's style also evolved. His slightly glossy paint and very fine grit sanding made his dolls look as though they were made out of clay or ceramic. Later, that smooth finish would make his traditional-style dolls stand out as well.

His first exposure to the traditional style came in 1998 at Powamuya, which is the first dance of the katsina cycle at Mùnqapi. It is often called the bean dance in reference to the bean sprouts attached to the gifts which the katsinam hand out.

> *"I noticed these old-style katsina dolls and thought,*
> *'Wow, that's nice! I never thought of trying those.*
> *I should give it a shot.'"*

He thought more about it and told his wife he was going to try some and see if he could sell them anywhere. "The first place I tried was Winter Sun in Flagstaff (page 87), and Phyllis really liked my work." After that first sale he began looking through old books for ideas and started experimenting with form and paint combinations. He prefers a mix of very diluted acrylics and *tuuma*. Many buyers, as well as other carvers, comment on his painting. He now enjoys both styles and trades off between carving the contemporary and traditional dolls and making his paintings and pottery.

The public also likes the way he paints his traditional-style dolls, which happens to be the most difficult part of the process for Jerold. "I try not to draw a straight line on my traditional-style dolls; I try to get it as shaky as I can. I'm so used to painting straight lines on my contemporary dolls that it's hard not to." We joked that he should drink a lot of coffee and smoke a pack of cigarettes before he carves to see if that helps.

HOOTE
(no English translation).
Winter Sun Trading Company.

Jerold doesn't mind visitors and teaches his children to respect all cultures, but he also feels that non-Indians are under-educated about the rules at Hopi. "If the non-Indians come here to our reservation, then they should abide by the rules," he said. "It only takes one to mess it up for everybody." However, once informed they are usually respectful. He gave an example of a curious tourist asking his brother questions at a dance. "He said to the woman, 'There are certain things I can tell you about it and certain things I cannot tell you about.' She said 'Oh, okay, I understand.'" He feels the majority of problems are due to lack of information. "That's one thing that should be done. They should be informed about what's where and where they can and can't walk, because they don't know."

> *"Tourists like seeing the plants and learning*
> *a little of how the Hopi live."*

The lifestyle is also a major appeal of Hopi. The farming, the breathtaking landscape, and the Hopi people themselves all contribute to something that's more than just a vacation. He believes tourists come to Hopi for an experience. Jerold doesn't mind sharing that experience. In fact, he feels it enriches other people's lives. "They have read about us, and when they visit the place and see a dance they go home happy and feel free."

Hahay'iwùuti
(no English translation).
Winter Sun Trading Company.

Clark Tenakhongva

Each room in Clark's modern house at the bottom of First Mesa is a different color in the Hopi paint scheme—everything from turquoise to pink—and every wall is covered with Clark's dolls. Some of the traditional-style dolls are twenty years old. He has a few pets, but rather than the "Rez mutt" one might expect, Clark's pet of choice is a parrot. This is one loud parrot.

Born and raised on the reservation, Clark had a familiar upbringing. He attended a boarding school, and eventually entered the military. He served for twelve years in the army and, during that time, he participated in the extraction of Panamanian strongman Manuel Noriega and was the only Hopi to serve during the Grenada conflict.

> *"I actually had bullets flying past my head.*
> *That was enough for me."*

The experience was enough to convince Clark to end his military career and head back to the reservation. Clark has carved off and on since he was twelve, but wanted to try something new. Now married and living at First Mesa, he took up pottery. His wife is a potter and Clark often helped her with her painting. He also made his own miniature pots with Hopi designs engraved on them. Eventually, out of respect, he says, he gave it up. Clark felt that this was a First Mesa craft and, being from Hotvela on Third Mesa, it wasn't his place to do pottery.

He began, instead, to carve contemporary-action dolls and sculptures. "I was carving what I refer to as the Michelangelo dolls, the more precise, detailed dolls. Being an artist already it wasn't hard for me to do. That went on until I accepted a job with the Hopi Police Department." Clark was offered a law enforcement position and worked in the justice system for seven years. He started as a police officer and worked his way up to tribal court advocate. He

OPPOSITE LEFT:
WAKASKATSINA *(Cow)*.
OPPOSITE CENTER:
PATRO *(Snipe)*.
OPPOSITE RIGHT:
PAATANGKATSINA *(Squash)*.
All Barbara Rice collection.

described this as being a lawyer, but without the degree. At one time or another he was everything from a prosecutor to a divorce lawyer.

Clark continued to carve in his spare time for extra cash and was doing well with it. He remembers selling his first doll to Tsakurshovi (page 27) in 1984—a very detailed piece. He thinks Joseph, the owner, gave him a hundred dollars for it. Joseph said he'd try to sell it and see how it goes. Soon, Clark was selling dolls primarily in the big shops in Sedona. One day he was laid off from his job and that was when he started carving on a full-time basis.

> *"I started getting into what they call 'old-style.' I call
> them 'traditional-style' because we never got away
> from them. That's the way they were always made and
> are still made today."*

Clark recounted the first time he was asked to do the traditional style. Joseph Day had been selling Clark's contemporary style for some time at Tsakurshovi and they had developed a good relationship. "He came down here to the house one day," Clark said, "and he saw all of these traditional dolls hanging on the walls and said, 'Where did you get all these dolls? Who made these?' 'I did,' I said. He kind of got mad at me and said, 'You know that I sell traditional dolls. Why don't you sell me these kind?'" So Clark started carving them to sell and Joseph bought everything he made.

Clark further defined his style and hit the Indian art circuit in 1994. The first show he entered was at the Santa Fe Indian Market. "That was one of the greatest years I can ever recall, because not only did I receive the 'best of' classification in my category, but I also won first, second, third, and best of division. I just kind of ran away with the whole show that year. I remember that the other carvers were kind of mad, like who's this new kid. The first time in the show winning like that. I couldn't believe it, because that was the first time I made money like that. I was not used to making a substantial amount of money from selling dolls."

The paint on Clark's dolls make them unique—they're unusually thick and almost bumpy. He doesn't use any sealant but uses a lot of

tuuma instead, which makes them difficult to rub off. He gets his pigments from all over the Southwest. "Traditional style to me is something that I created with my own hands, and I either use natural pigments or plant dyes."

Sticking to the basics is Clark's philosophy. "A hundred years ago they didn't have these modernized tools, but in the 1950s and 1960s a touristy trend of dolls came about. They went into a trend of making dolls in a more intricate style. That's not how it's supposed to be. A doll is supposed to simply portray a certain kind of katsina. It's a spirit. It doesn't have to be to the point that it's really detailed, as long as it's basic in the form, meaning the head and body parts." For Clark, this is less of an art form and more of a religious act. Because of his strong religious convictions, he doesn't believe women should be carving. He also believes a carver should speak Hopi. "If you don't speak and understand it," he says, "you don't know the significance behind it, and that's important."

"A katsina, whether it's a runner katsina or a squash, whatever it is, it's identifiable by the head."

Once known for carving very large heads on his dolls, Clark has toned them down a bit and is carving them more proportionately. "My grandfather would tell me the main thing you focus on in a katsina doll is the head, so that's where I was going with the big heads. Then a non-Hopi Indian who makes it a habit of imitating traditional-style dolls started copying my dolls with the big heads. I had to change because I don't want anyone else doing what I'm doing. That's why I became more precise."

Clark tries very hard to maintain his traditions and raise his children in accordance with them. He insists that they help in tending his fields, and dinner-table conversation is always in Hopi. Even though 60 percent of Clark's income goes to saving for his children's college education, he knows his children will also have knowledge of their Hopi culture. "My grandfather told me do it the right way and stick with the traditional system. When I first started carving he'd tell me to carve belly-acher dolls. I was good carving the one-piece, stylized dolls, but something within me told me, 'Go back to what's good for you.' I would not be comfortable carving a one-piece doll now, because I would be going away from the religious beliefs of how they're supposed to be carved. Within my heart I believe this is the right way."

MASTOPKATSINA
(no English translation).
Barbara Rice collection.

CLIFFORD TORIVIO

The yellow exterior of Clifford Torivio's 1970s apartment complex near the high school, with its spray-painted apartment numbers, looked out of place in the desert landscape. His mother answered the door and I think she was surprised. "Who's there?," Clifford asked. "It's some white guy," she said in Hopi. I think she was even more surprised when she realized I understood her. She returned to her cooking and I went upstairs to see Clifford. He was in his bedroom carving and watching television. I took a seat on the bed by the window.

A quiet, mild-mannered artist, Clifford is a member of the Water Clan from Songòopavi, and his Hopi name is *Honhoya*, or Young Bear. His mother is Hopi and his father is Acoma. During our talk he made a point to thank everyone (from his mother to various traders) who had encouraged or guided him along his artistic path. A humble man, he gives a lot of credit to others and often fails to mention that his success is also due to a natural talent and practiced skill.

A traditional Hopi, Clifford speaks his language and is trying to make sure his kids will speak it as well. "I never used to speak Hopi," he said. "I always used to just talk Anglo, *Pahaana*. Then I started asking my mom what's the proper way to say a Hopi word." Now he primarily speaks English only when he goes to town. "Practice your language, your tradition, and your values. At some villages these things are dying out."

> *"I believe in giving my dolls a home where someone will take care of them."*

Clifford first tried carving at a very young age, but his mother let him know right away that this wasn't acceptable and he would have to wait until he was initiated. The next time he picked up a knife was when he was seventeen. As with many Hopi he learned by watching his father. The Acoma also practice a katsina religion,

OPPOSITE LEFT:
HILILI
(no English translation).
Jonathan S. Day collection.
OPPOSITE CENTER:
HEMISKATSINA
(no English translation).
Jonathan S. Day collection.
OPPOSITE RIGHT:
WAKASKATSINA *(Cow).*
Barbara Rice collection.

KIPOKKOYEMSI
(Warrior Mudhead).
Winter Sun Trading Company.

though their dolls are different and rarely seen for sale. Soon, he began getting into the one-piece contemporary style and specialized in miniatures. However, this wasn't his only source of income. He was also a forest fire-fighter on an all-Indian crew. In the summers, he battled blazes all over the county and in the off-season he carved.

It wasn't until 1996 that Clifford tried the traditional-style dolls. Bendrew Atokuku (page 18), his clan brother and best friend since childhood, introduced him to this resurgent style. "We used to kick back here and carve and watch TV. First, he asked me to teach him the contemporary, but instead he taught me the old style. He told me how to cut them. At first I started out with flat dolls. I never tried the full-figured dolls out of respect for Bendrew. I didn't want to interfere with his artwork."

To this day, Clifford still makes the flat dolls in great quantity and variety. Soon, Bendrew encouraged him to carve the bigger dolls and, with his blessing, he delved into the full-size dolls. The first full-size doll he made was a parrot. He sold it for twenty-five dollars at the flea market. "My mom really likes them. She says this is how they made them a long time ago before they got all *kwiivi* [finicky] and perfect."

Switching back and forth between the contemporary and the traditional, the style he carves depends on his mindset. As for which katsina he carves, this also depends on a lot of factors. He likes to make the dolls that nobody makes anymore: the older ones. Often he tries a new katsina in the traditional style first, and if he likes the outcome he'll try a contemporary miniature. Other times it's up to the customer. "People that I sell to give me ideas of what they want. There are certain katsinam we have that can represent certain people. Like this cop up in Michigan. He's an enforcer, so I made him a Hilili, which is also an enforcer."

Clifford and Bendrew are unique in that they gather many of their own feathers. The two often go down to the reservoir in Tuba City and hunt for birds. He says as soon as he gets a bird he knows what kind of dolls he will make with them. Clifford is always experimenting to find what works for him and enjoys working with natural materials. His paints are a mix of ancient and modern. "I tried pure pigments but it would chip off." (Clifford applies his paints thick.) For this reason, he now mixes acrylic with *tuuma* to stabilize the coat and avoid chipping and flaking.

"It really brings me back home when I'm putting on the real feathers. They [traditional-style dolls] seem more alive than the contemporary."

Adamant about respecting his culture, Clifford acknowledges that carving is more than a way to earn money. He always asks his mother if he's allowed to make a certain *Mongkatsina,* or chief katsina. "I believe that I have respect for the Hopi culture. I don't want to break laws and suffer or have regrets in the future. I'm young, yet and I don't want to be crippled when I'm getting old because they say they [the katsinam] do things to you."

He's also careful around his kids. "When they ask me about the dolls I say I'm just copying what the katsinam make. They make the real ones and I'm just copying them." Preserving his culture and its secrets is very important to him and he feels some books do more harm than good. "Nowadays, it's gone too far and they're bringing out the secrets of the Hopi: the sacred stuff we're not supposed to be telling. It's in all the books. My son, who's not initiated, checked out a book at the library about this little boy who got initiated. I was really disappointed. I guess the Hopi kids want to know about Hopi and it's just out of curiosity."

Kyarkatsina *(Parrot).*
Winter Sun Trading Company.

BERTRAM TSAVADAWA

Bertram Tsavadawa was born on the Colorado River Indian Tribes Reservation near Parker, Arizona. This intertribal reservation on the California–Arizona border is home to Native Americans from a variety of tribal backgrounds. Bertram's mother is Hopi and his father is Hualapai. He and his family lived in Riverside, California, where his parents were employed at a local boarding school. When he was seven his parents separated, and Bertram and his mother moved back to Hopi. They settled in Old Orayvi and started a new life.

> *"My grandfather was the one who said*
> *this is how the dolls should be looking."*

We talked at his wife's home in Songòopavi. He was sitting on a stool in front of the wood stove, busily carving a *Masaw Mana* for a special order. He's a full-time carver, but his beginnings are in painting. He first saw the traditional style at the Hopi Tricentennial in 1980 when some of Bertram's paintings had been selected to be part of a related show in Mesa, Arizona.

"We caught a ride down with Michael Kabotie, and Manfred [Susunkewa] was there demonstrating," he said. "They had this trough set up in the back room where you could pan for gold. I think it was fool's gold though. Manfred was situated back there." They struck up a conversation and, though not about the dolls, it was the first time Bertram had seen the style. Today, he remembers the impact the dolls made on him. He liked that they were different, but didn't consider carving them for another eleven years.

Instead, he focused on school and painting. In grade school and high school he had won numerous awards at the Museum of Northern Arizona, and later attended the prominent Institute of American Indian Art in Santa Fe, New Mexico. He liked the school, he says. The teachers were all artists themselves and the majority of the staff was Native American. He lived in the dormitories and

OPPOSITE LEFT:
ÀHOOLI
(no English translation).

OPPOSITE CENTER:
KIISA *(Chicken Hawk).*

OPPOSITE RIGHT:
MONGWU
(Great Horned Owl).
All Barbara Rice collection.

SIVU'IKWIWTAQA
(no English translation).
Barbara Rice collection.

enjoyed the change of living in a city. "We all used to walk downtown and go to tons of gallery openings. It was fun, and there was always free drinks and food." Bertram majored in museum studies, but after a year he decided to switch to two-dimensional art and concentrate on the finer points of painting.

Initially, Bertram found the market for paintings discouraging. He sold to a few shops and then his uncle got him into the Pueblo Grande market. Then, in 1991, he was invited to attend The Folk Life Festival at the Smithsonian. While there he was given the opportunity to tour their katsina doll collections, which he thought were "old and real crude looking." Bertram had carved his first doll when he was twelve and he continued to carve part time. He ususally carved flat dolls, and learned by hanging around other carvers and "trying what they were doing." However, he still didn't try the traditional style for another year.

After his second year at the institute Bertram returned to Hopi to take some time off from school. It was intended to be a short break, but it turned into a long one, and it was during this short break that he changed from painting to carving.

"You can hang traditional dolls and it gives your
house a more spiritual feel. . . . When they're hanging
up in a house on the rafters it's like they're spirits
floating to watch the people and watch the children."

In 1991, Bertram and Wallace Hyeoma (page 46) spent a lot of their time sitting on a bench outside of Tsakurshovi (page 27), carving. At that time the store had only a few traditional-style dolls: by Manfred Susunkewa. No one else was doing that kind of carving yet. The owner, Joseph, showed him the doll and he decided to try an old-style flat doll. When he finally tried his first full-figure, traditional-style doll, he was still learning and experimenting with different paints.

He also tried different carving methods, including electric carving tools. "I wanted to see how it would look using a Dremel, but it didn't really grab me." From then on he only used hand tools, knives, and files, and found this new style both satisfying and challenging. "I liked them because they were a breakaway from my painting," he said.

*"All the materials that I use are more or less
from the earth: feathers from the birds, horse hair,
corn husk, cotton string, and even leather."*

Over the years, Bertram's carving has really taken off. Appearing in many museum shows and native markets, and represented in a handful of galleries, his dolls are a hot seller and mail orders from collectors keep him very busy. I asked him why he thought they were such a hit with tourists. "A lot of writing has been done, about Hopi especially, and Anglos are fascinated because they don't know all the meanings behind it. These are teaching tools to show people different spirits." He also feels the pastel colors are very appealing. "I also like them because they show a little of the history and because they are part of our culture, but the ones who really like them are the people that have been coming out here for a while."

Bertram still carves full time but is now starting to get back into paintings. He showed me one of his new pieces—petroglyph designs painted with mineral pigments. "I thought it would be neat to try the same paints I use on the dolls in two-dimensional art." By the look of his first attempt I think this new avenue is full of promise.

Sootukwnangw
(Star Katsina).
Barbara Rice collection.

GARY TSO

I've known Gary Tso for many years; he works at Tsakurshovi on Second Mesa (page 27). I occasionally work there as well, and so we've had the chance to talk at great length. The day I interviewed him he was working and busy carving the dolls to be photographed for this book. To see five of Gary's dolls at once is unusual. He sells his dolls the minute he makes them, usually to tourists that come in the shop and see a work in progress, so he rarely has more than one on hand.

> *"Most of the time tourists think the traditional-style [dolls] are the contemporary because they have never seen them before. They think the ones with all the action and detail are traditional."*

Gary's father is Navajo, his mother Hopi. The early part of his childhood was spent with his grandparents at Grand Falls, thirty miles north of Flagstaff, while his mother attended Northern Arizona University. He doesn't remember any of it now, but his mother tells him he spoke nothing but Navajo until he was three. His mother took a break from school and they moved back to the Hopi Reservation. When he was six he spoke Hopi and didn't speak English at all until he started school.

Growing up half Navajo at Hopi wasn't easy for Gary. Even though his mother is full-blooded Hopi, which means that he is con- sidered 100 percent Hopi, people still gave him a rough time. This even affected his religious practices for a while, but he eventually became actively involved in the Hopi religion. Today, he is a dedicated family man and attends his wife's kiva in Supawlavi.

Gary was interested in art at school and painted a little. When he was twelve his mother decided it was time for him to carve. She sent him to see his godfather, Delbridge Honanie. "I remember he gave me a real soft piece of wood. The first doll I ever carved was a mudhead. I didn't really carve it because that wood was so soft. I

OPPOSITE LEFT:
TOHÒOKATSINA
(Mountain Lion).
Anonymous collector.

OPPOSITE CENTER:
HONÀN KATSINA *(Badger).*
Hannah Honanie collection.

OPPOSITE RIGHT:
AVATSHOYA *(Corn Boy).*
Roxanna Vuskalns collection.

SIVUTOOTOVI
(Black Fly).
Anonymous collector.

ended up using a rasp to shape most of it." His mother took him into town to sell it at the curio shop she worked at while attending Northern Arizona University. He sold it for fifteen dollars. That was the last doll he carved for a long time. Because it was so hard and it took so much time away from his playtime, he didn't stick with it.

Eventually Gary's focus turned from playtime to his education. He attended The Orme School, an exclusive college preparatory school located on a forty-thousand-acre central Arizona ranch, and received a full scholarship to Lewis and Clark College in Portland, Oregon, for cross-country running. However, instead of college he decided on a completely different path. One day he decided to join the Marine Corps. "I woke up, got a bottle of water, and started to walk to Flagstaff; I hitched a ride ten miles outside of Kiqötsmovi. I went to the recruiting office, signed the papers, and walked to NAU to tell my mom. She was pretty upset." After a four-year tour in the marines he returned to school and earned an associate's degree in graphic design and advertising. Eventually he plans to complete a bachelor's degree in liberal arts.

After school he moved back to the reservation and managed various restaurants there until 1996, when he began working at Tsakurshovi. That was when he first started to carve again, and he tried the traditional style. "I think people are drawn to traditional-style dolls because they are truer to the real function of katsina dolls. They are very simple and, in my opinion, people are looking for more simplicity in their lives." Wallace Hyeoma (page 46) was working at the trading post, and Gary credits him with reintroducing him to carving.

The first traditional doll Gary carved was a *Tsakwaina* katsina, the *wu'ya* (ancestor) of the Mustard Clan. Manuel Denet Chavarria, Jr. (page 22), had one for sale at Tsakurshovi. Gary really liked it, so he tried one.

Gary started with the traditional-style dolls, but he also tried the contemporary and says he enjoys both. Still, he doesn't carve the contemporary as much anymore. "I used to be able to look at a piece of wood and really plan it out in my head, and all of a sudden it just turned off." He figures this ability will return someday and is just as happy to carve traditional-style dolls in the meantime, though he misses the challenge of the action dolls.

"The left-handed katsina is a hunter, a warrior, an
artist, and a thief. I guess I identify with that because
I've been all those things at one time in my life."

Gary is well known for his rendition of his favorite katsina, the left-handed hunter. He even has one tattooed on his back. He says he likes carving lefties so much because he is a lefty. Because Hopi is a right-handed society, he had a more difficult time adjusting—not just to being a Hopi because of his background, but because he's left-handed. In a social dance the rattle is always held in the right hand, and other dance items are held in the left hand. Except for the *Suyang'evu,* or the left-handed katsina.

Gary believes non-Indians should be welcome on the reservation and at ceremonies. "I think it is wrong to close the dances," he said. "The katsinam are here for all of us. My mother always told me what her grandfather told her: Each person represents a cloud, and if you keep some people out you keep clouds away. A katsina dance is a ritualized prayer in which everybody takes part. You listen to the music and you understand what they're singing about. You are, in a sense, praying yourself. If you keep people away you'll always have that stigma in the back of your mind that it's not going to work."

Gary also runs a successful tour company. He offers visitors a rare insight into Hopi life by allowing them to visit archaeological and petroglyph sites, and meet Hopi artists. An avid mountain biker, he can even take you on the ride of your life if you're up to it. In my opinion, it's the best way to really see the reservation.

"I see this stuff out here all the time," Gary said. "I like it and I understand the beauty in it. I think that the *Pahaanas* are attracted to the difference in the environment." No matter what it is, Gary will be certain to dazzle you with his knowledge of Hopi history and make sure you have a blast.

AFTERWORD

I know most of the carvers in this book well enough to call them friends. Still, the context and framework in which I conducted my interviews addressed issues I had never talked to them about before. Along the way I made several personal discoveries that I had never considered about the Hopi carving world. This reinforces my motto: I am only a witness to this culture, not a participant.

One such discovery is how open-minded they are toward non-Indians, which gives me great hope for the survival of this art form and the future of Hopi and non-Indian relations. I believe that most Hopis, though a little wary at first, judge all non-Indians on an indi-vidual basis. They welcome visitors no matter their race, and it is the sum of our words and actions on a personal level that determines their opinion of us. All they want is courtesy and respect; if you give it to them, they'll give it to you.

The preference by most of the artists for making their own paints is fascinating. Natural paints allow them to grab a piece of their past, pull it into the present, and preserve it for the future. It is one way they get away from modern inventions—even if only for a brief time—and imagine what life and carving was like for their grandfathers. Whether they are gathering the materials, grinding in just the right amount of *tuuma,* or viewing the final product, making paint is one way that they hold on to the past.

OPPOSITE:
A rare look inside the ancient village of Walpi on First Mesa.

The relationships between the carvers is also interesting and it is a phenomenon I call the "trickle-down effect" of carving. Most of the carvers of this style can trace their roots back to three or four carvers. Those uncles, brothers, or friends shared their knowledge with someone, each in turn taught the next, and at this rate the exponential nature of this process will produce a bright group of future artists. The revival of the traditional style is still in its infancy and what comes next may surprise us all.

APPENDIX
MUSEUMS, SHOPS, AND TRADING POSTS

BUFFALO BARRY'S INDIAN ARTS
132 School Street
Boylston, MA 01505
bbia@gis.net

Barry does not have a storefront and sells most of his art through the mail and the Internet on ebay.com. A private dealer since 1987, he specializes in antiquities and keeps an inventory of one hundred or more Early Traditional, Late Traditional, and New Traditional style katsina dolls. Drop him a letter or e-mail and he may be able to find what you're looking for. Barry is also available to lecture for student groups, schools, and museums. See page 45 for more information.

CASE TRADING POST: WHEELWRIGHT MUSEUM OF THE AMERICAN INDIAN
704 Camino Lejo
Santa Fe, NM 87502
(505) 982-4636
www.collectorsguide.com/sf/m001.htm

Housed in the lower level of the Wheelwright Museum, an eight-sided building inspired by a traditional Navajo hogan, Case Trading Post has one of the finest collections of contemporary and traditional American Indian art in the Southwest. The creaky wood floor, vigas ceiling, and shelves stocked with pottery, jewelry, rugs, and katsina dolls gives this charming shop the look and feel of a turn-of-the-century trading post. Case represents a wide variety of New Traditional style katsina doll carvers (Philbert Honanie, Manuel Denet Chavarria, Clark Tenakhongva, Clifford Torivio, Bendrew Atokuku, Ferris Satala, and Chris Gashwazra) and stocks an excellent selection of books on American Indian art and culture.

HAGGARD'S TRADING POST
8340 East Washington Street
Indianapolis, IN 46219
(317) 897-8065

Founded in 1974, Haggard's Trading Post is located in the heart of Hoosier country, but specializes in Southwest Native American art. Twice a year Dick and Kate Haggard travel to New Mexico and hand pick all of the art they buy: jewelry, pottery, Navajo rugs, baskets, and katsina dolls. Be sure to ask about their large collection of Hopi traditional dolls, which have included several of the carvers featured in this book (Manuel Denet Chavarria, Wallace Hyeoma, Vernon Mansfield, and Jerold Sekletstewa) and others.

HEARD MUSEUM OF NATIVE CULTURES AND ART

22 E. Monte Vista Road
Phoenix, AZ 85004
(602) 252-8848
www.heard.org

Nestled amid skyscrapers in downtown Phoenix, the cozy, Spanish Colonial-style museum is world renown for its Southwest culture exhibits and specializes in American Indian art. The museum's permanent collection contains pottery, weavings, basketry, and paintings; there is even an entire room devoted to Hopi and Zuni katsina dolls. Also, the gift shop carries a good selection of New Traditional style katsina dolls by a variety of carvers (Manfred Susunkewa, Walter Howato, Manuel Denet Chavarria, Larry Melendez, Fred Ross, Clark Tenakhongva, and others) as well as a great selection of books on American Indian culture. An anthropology library is also available for further research.

THE HOPI HOUSE
GRAND CANYON NATIONAL PARK (SOUTH RIM)

P.O. Box 97
Grand Canyon, AZ 86023
(520) 638-3458

Built in 1905 with the aid of Hopi craftsmen, this historic, sandstone building sits at the edge of the Grand Canyon's South Rim. The building itself is an attraction, which is modeled after Hopi dwellings in Orayvi (Oraibi), Arizona, and it has served as a residence and store for American Indians and their crafts. The first floor is stocked with pottery, baskets, fetishes, rugs, jewelry, and souvenirs. Upstairs in the gallery, among display cases and shelves of contemporary and traditional American Indian art, is a diverse collection of New Traditional style dolls.

LEFT-HANDED HUNTER TOURS

P.O. Box 434
Second Mesa, AZ 86043
(520) 734-2567
LHHunter58@Hotmail.com

A great way to see the Hopi Reservation is with Gary Tso as your guide. He can customize a tour around your schedule and interests. Whatever the size of your group Gary will be sure to show you a great time. Gary also sells his New Traditional style katsina dolls. See page 102 for more information.

THE MONONGYA GALLERY

P.O. Box 287
Old Oraibi, AZ 86039
(520) 734-2344

In business for over twenty years, The Monongya Gallery is one of the largest sellers of Hopi art and crafts on the Hopi Reservation. It is located on Third Mesa just outside the village of Old Oraibi on Arizona 264, which is the oldest continuously inhabited community in the United States (A.D. 1150). The gallery carries a large selection of locally made art and crafts in the more modern styles as well as a limited selection of New Traditional style katsina dolls by Manuel Denet Chavarria, Larry Melendez, Cliffton Lomayaktewa, Fred Ross, and others, many of whom are newer to the style. In addition, the gallery has an intertribal room where it sells Navajo, Zuni, and Acoma art.

MUSEUM OF NORTHERN ARIZONA

3001 N. Fort Valley Road
Flagstaff, AZ 86001
(520) 779-1703
www.musnaz.org

In the pines of Flagstaff on the way to the Grand Canyon, the MNA is the perfect introduction to the arts, Native American cultures, and natural sciences (anthropology, biology, geology) of the Colorado Plateau. The museum's nine galleries (five galleries with permanent collections and four with changing exhibits) on natural and native history include the Hopi Kiva room and Hopi Jewelry Gallery. There is also an exhibit in the Babbitt Gallery showcasing part of the museum's extensive katsina doll collection with interpretation of the katsina's role in Hopi culture. If you're in the Flagstaff area May through September, don't miss the annual sales exhibition "Enduring Creations: Masterworks of Native American Art," which showcases fine Indian artwork from the Hopi, Navajo, Pai, and Zuni tribes. Also, check out the Hopi Marketplace—an annual event that usually falls around the Fourth of July. Be sure to stop at the bookstore, gift shop, and gallery. The gift shop sells New Traditional style katsina dolls by Clark Tenakhongva, Manfred Susunkewa, Manuel Denet Chavarria, and others.

OLD TERRITORIAL SHOP

7220 E. Main Street
Scottsdale, AZ 85251
(480) 945-5432

Opened in 1969, the Old Territorial Shop is the oldest Indian trading post on Main Street in Old Town Scottsdale, and it is recommended by museums for the authenticity and quality of the art it sells. "Old Arizona" are the words that best describe the shop's rustic interior, which is complete with wooden floors and walls, and the shelves are stocked with some of the finest modern and antique American Indian art (baskets, pottery, rugs, jewelry, katsina dolls, fetishes, etc.) available. In fact, several of the New Traditional style carvers mentioned in this book (Fred Ross, Larry Melendez, Manuel Denet Chavarria, and Philbert Honanie) are represented here. Also, the shop's friendly owners take pride in educating consumers about the art that they sell. See page 51 for more information.

SACRED MOUNTAIN TRADING POST

HC33, Box 436
Flagstaff, AZ 86004
(520) 679-2255

Located 20 miles north of Flagstaff on U.S. 89A, the Sacred Mountain Trading Post was used as a film site for Dennis Hopper's 1969 cult-film classic Easy Rider. Today, the trading post, which was founded in 1960, is stocked with a wide variety of katsina dolls, pottery, baskets, and jewelry from many Southwestern Indian tribes. The art is housed in forty-year-old display cases that sit on wooden floors, which creak under every step. The trading post's New Traditional style katsina doll collection usually includes carvings by Clifford Torivio. The owner, Bill Beaver, lives behind the trading post in a Hopi-style sandstone house.

TSAKURSHOVI
P.O. Box 234
Second Mesa, AZ 86043
(520) 734-2478

Located a mile-and-a-half east of the Hopi Cultural Center on Highway 264, this funky, little trading post doesn't have fancy track lighting or wall to wall carpet, but it does offer one of the most unique and complete selections of traditional Hopi art, crafts, and cultural items found anywhere. Walking into Tsakurshovi is like stepping into an old-time trading post whose walls, ceiling, and roof beams are covered with baskets, katsina dolls, bows and arrows, rabbit sticks, and ceremonial textiles. There are also a lot of other items, which are unidentifiable to most non-Hopi visitors: jars of mineral pigments, stacks of cottonwood root, gourds for rattles, deer hooves, culinary ash, and traditional herbs. The staff at Tsakurshovi (all Hopi artists) does an excellent job of not only explaining the materials and techniques used in the production of Hopi arts and crafts, but also their cultural context. Most of the carvers mentioned in this book have dolls for sale at Tsakurshovi. See page 27 for more information.

WINTER SUN TRADING COMPANY
107 N. San Francisco Street, Suite 1
Flagstaff, AZ 86001
(520) 774-2884
www.wintersun.com

Located in historic downtown Flagstaff, Winter Sun maintains the second largest selection of New Traditional style dolls as well as a huge selection of jewelry, herbs, teas, and beauty products. The smell of two hundred different herbs stacked to the ceiling in glass jars, a giant juniper staircase, hardwood floors, antique display cases, sandstone walls, and the friendly, informative staff make shopping at Winter Sun an enjoyable experience. Also, owner Phyllis Hogan creates an opportunity to meet carvers every Fourth of July weekend. She holds an annual "Preserving a Tradition" carving exhibition. Several artists mentioned in this book (Danny Denet, Bertram Tsavadawa, Tay Polequaptewa, Manuel Denet Chavarria, Philbert Honanie, and Fred Ross) come to the store to carve and discuss their work with the public. See page 83 for more information.

GLOSSARY OF TERMS

AWTA: A bow and arrow.

AYA: A rattle.

DREMEL: An electric power tool used in the carving of some contemporary katsina dolls.

HAHAY'IWÙUTI: The first doll given to an infant.

HONNGÀAPI: Bear root.

KATSIN TIHU: A Hopi katsina doll.

KATSIN TITHU: Plural of katsin tihu.

KATSINA: A spirit being in the Hopi world that is represented at ceremonies.

KATSINAM: Plural of katsina.

KIVA: An underground ceremonial chamber.

KWIIVÍ: Finicky.

PAAHO: A prayer stick or prayer feathers.

PAAKO: Cottonwood root.

PAHAANA: A legendary, lost white Hopi brother and a term for Anglos.

PIIKI: Rolled, wafer-thin bread used in Hopi ceremonies.

PUTSQA TIHU: A simple, flat doll.

SA'LAKO: A kachina ceremony that takes place approximately once a decade during Niman and several of the katsinam that participate in it.

SAKWATOOTSI: Hopi blue moccasins.

SUMIVIKI: A traditional Hopi sweet.

TOVOKÌMPI (BULLROARER): A piece of cottonwood root that is tied to a string and swung in a circular motion, making a sound like wind to help bring rain.

TUUMA: A white clay that is mixed with pigment for paint.

WU'YA: Ancestral spirit of a clan.

GLOSSARY OF PLACE NAMES

All of the Hopi villages mentioned in the text, with the exception of Keams Canyon, use the Hopi spelling. Keams Canyon is excluded because it was established by the federal government. The following entries include the approximate translation and Hopi meaning.

PAAQAVI: Bacavi, which means the place of the jointed reed.

HANOKI (TEWA): Hano, which means Tewa home.

HOTVELA: Hotevilla, which means juniper slope. It is a distortion of hó'atuela, which was what the location was called before the village was established because it led to a spring.

KEAMS CANYON: Pongsikvi, which means government town. The English name comes from Varker Keams who was a Navajo agent. It is the location for the first government school at Hopi (1887).

KIQÖTSMOVI: Kykotsmovi, which means ruin hill.

MUSANGNUVI: Mishongnovi, which means the other of the two sandstone columns remains standing.

MÙNQAPI: Moenkopi, which means place of running water.

ORAYVI: Oraibi comes from Sip-oraibi, which means something that has been solidified or in Hopi mythology, a place where the earth was made solid.

POLACCA: Polacca, which means butterfly. The village was established in 1890 by Tom Polacca, a Tewa Indian from Hanoki.

SUPAWLAVI: Shipaulovi, which means place of mosquitos. The translation refers to a clan living there now (formerly at Homolovi), which was abandoned because of mosquitos.

SONGÒOPAVI: Shungopavi, which means a place of chumoa (a kind of grass or reed).

SITSOM'OVI: Sichomovi, which means place of the wild currant bush mound.

TUBA CITY: Tuba City, or Qötsatuwa, which means white sand is named after the Hopi leader who established nearby Mùnqapi (Moenkopi). His name was T Ivi, which was pronounced by local Mormons as Tuba and Tocobi.

WÀLPI: Walpi, which means place of the gap.

Information for this list was obtained by consulting *Arizona's Names: X Marks the Spot* by Byrd Howell Granger and *Hopi Dictionary=Hopìikwa Lavàytutuveni: A Hopi–English Dictionary of the Third Mesa Dialect* compiled by the Hopi Dictionary Project.

Selected Reading

Adams, E. Charles. *The Origin and Development of the Pueblo Katsina Cult.* Tucson: University of Arizona Press, 1991.
   The history and development of the Katsina religion and its function in Hopi and Pueblo society. Emphasis is on the archaeological record as evidence.

Breunig, Robert. *Hopi Kachina Dolls.* Flagstaff: Museum of Northern Arizona, 1992.
   A very good introduction to both form and function as well as the Hopi ceremonial cycle. Includes interviews with carvers as well as advice on collecting.

Eddington, Patrick and Susan Makov. *The Trading Post Guidebook: Where to Find the Trading Posts, Galleries, Auctions, Artists, and Museums of the Four Corners Region.* Flagstaff: Northland Publishing, 1995.
   A valuable source for contacting, visiting, and purchasing from the Native American arts community of the Four Corners region, including those out-of-the-way places.

Erickson, Jon T. *Kachinas: An Evolving Hopi Art Form.* Phoenix: The Heard Museum Press, 1977.
   A good visual presentation of the evolution of carving styles plus some historical background.

Fewkes, Jesse Walter. *Hopi Kachinas, Drawn By Native Artists.* Smithsonian Institution Bureau of American Ethnology Annual Report, 1903. Reprint, Mineola: Dover Publications Inc., 1985.
   There is both correct and incorrect information in this volume, which was one of the first attempts to collect the names and document the appearance of Hopi katsinam. Most of the katsinam portrayed in this book still appear today and the lack of substantial changes in their appearance is remarkable.

Jacka, Lois Essary and Jerry Jacka. *Art of the Hopi: Contemporary Journeys on Ancient Pathways.* Flagstaff: Northland Publishing, 1993.
A vibrant and award-winning overview of Hopi paintings, baskets, jewelry, katsina dolls, and pottery.

James, Harry C. *Pages from Hopi History.* Tucson: University of Arizona Press, 1996.
A very good overview of Hopi history from 1540 (the date of first European contact) to the present. The author spent fifty years gathering this material.

Page, Susanne and Jake Page. *Hopi.* New York: Abrams, 1994.
Unlike most authors, Jake and Susanne Page were invited to do this book by the Hopis and this gave them photographic and other kinds of access that outsiders normally don't have. Susanne's beautiful photographs make this the ultimate coffee-table book on Hopi, and the excellent text on contemporary Hopi life gives it substance.

Roberts, David. *In Search of the Old Ones: Exploring the Anasazi World of the Southwest.* New York: Simon & Schuster, 1996.
The author takes all of the current archaeological theories about what was happening in the Southwest a thousand years ago and combines them with the Hopi and Pueblo points of view. A valuable book for understanding the ancestral Hopi world.

Schaafsma, Polly. *Kachinas in the Pueblo World.* Albuquerque: University of New Mexico Press, 1994.
This indispensable book includes fourteen papers, which were presented at a seminar entitled "World View and Ritual: Kachinas in the Pueblo World," and represents views from a wide variety of scholars—both Anglo and Indian. The paper by J. J. Brody is of particular interest to traditional-doll collectors.

Secakuku, Alph H. *Following the Sun and Moon: Hopi Kachina Tradition.* Flagstaff: Northland Publishing in cooperation with the Heard Museum, 1995.

> *The first book on katsinam authored by a Hopi. In addition to the excellent text, the photographs are of dolls in the Heard Museum's collection and alone are worth the price of the book.*

Teiwes, Helga. *Kachina Dolls: The Art of Hopi Carvers.* Tucson: University of Arizona Press, 1991.

> *This book covers the historical background and market forces that created the contemporary Hopi katsina doll. It also includes the techniques, styles, and biographical information of twenty-seven different carvers.*

Whiteley, Peter M. *Paaqavi (Bacavi): Journey to Reed Springs.* Flagstaff: Northland Publishing, 1988.

> *The story of the social, political, and cultural turmoil that led to the civil war at Orayvi (Oraibi) at the turn of the century, which resulted in the founding of three additional Hopi villages.*

Wright, Barton. *Hopi Kachinas: The Complete Guide to Collecting Kachina Dolls.* Flagstaff: Northland Publishing, 1977.

> *A highly readable, comprehensive guide to Hopi katsina dolls, including buying tips.*

Yava, Albert. *Big Falling Snow: A Tewa-Hopi Indian's Life and Times and the History and Traditions of His People.* Albuquerque: University of New Mexico Press, 1992.

> *A Hopi autobiography that deals with the cultural conflict that occurred as a result of the establishment of federal authority over the Hopi.*

ACKNOWLEDGMENTS

I would like to thank all of the artists in this book along with their families and all of the other Hopis who helped with this project. It is only with their help and advice that this book was possible.

I wish to thank all of my families—real, imagined, and surrogate—for their support: Dad and Janice, Mom and Alan, Phyllis, Kate, Barbara, Duke, and Beany. Thanks to Barry Walsh and Tryntje VanNess Seymour for their advice. Thanks to Barbara Rice for opening her home and collection for use in this book. Thanks to Winter Sun in Flagstaff and Tsakurshovi on Second Mesa for allowing me to borrow many of the dolls featured in this book. Thanks to Ed Wade at the Musueum of Northern Arizona in Flagstaff, Bill Gobus, Owen Seumptewa, Jerry and Lois Jacka, and Alston and Deborah Neal at the Old Territorial Shop in Scottsdale. Thanks to Stephanie Bucholz for making my dream a reality and for all of the encouragement and guidance. Thanks to Jennifer Schaber and the staff at Northland for the extra effort.

Finally, I would like to give special thanks to Kimberly Fox for the prodding and encouragement, which helped me finish this book.

INDEX

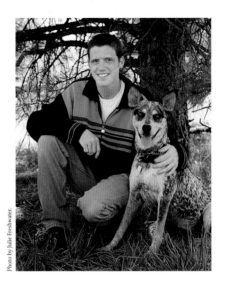

Photo by Julie Freshwater.

ABOUT THE AUTHOR

JONATHAN S. DAY was born in Flagstaff, Arizona, and is a second generation Indian trader. He grew up on the East Coast, but spent every summer on and around the Hopi Reservation. He was seven when he sold his first katsina doll for the Winter Sun Trading Company in Flagstaff. His career in Indian art continued at Tsakurshovi, a trading post on the Hopi Reservation owned by his father Joseph Day and his Hopi stepmother Janice. Later, Jonathan managed the Winter Sun Trading Company gallery for many years. Today, he lives in Flagstaff with his dog Isau'u where he continues to trade Katsina dolls; he is also an artist, consultant, and lecturer.